"This book, based on so much experie[nce]... [is] tremendously useful for millions of peopl[e]... [whose trust]
has been damaged. I found important i[nsights every-]
where."   —Pepper Schwart[z]

"If you want to find your way back to the people you love, this book
is a must-read. It offers a step-by-step map for rebuilding trust and
helping you find peace within."
          —Michele Weiner-Davis, author of *Divorce Busting*

"Mira Kirshenbaum gives us hope when the inevitable crises of betrayal besiege our most important relationships. With profound clarity and sensitivity, she guides us on a path toward surprisingly
effective healing."   —Rabbi Ted Falcon, PhD, spiritual therapist
          and coauthor of *Religion Gone Astray*

"Practical and helpful . . . a complete guide to rebuilding damaged
trust. Kirshenbaum shows us how hurts and challenges people struggle with can be overcome. A convincingly hopeful book to overcome
the despair of mistrust."
          —Eva Fogelman, PhD, author of the Pulitzer Prize
          nominee *Conscience and Courage*

"Mira Kirshenbaum is a steady guide through the muddy waters of
heartbreak and betrayal, offering sound strategies for making good
decisions in tough times."   —Dr. Dorothy Firman, author *Engaging Life:*
          Living Well with Chronic Illness

"A path-breaking book on restoring trust in relationships. A wonderful read based on deeply felt experiences."
          —Janis Abrahms Spring, PhD, author of *How Can I Forgive You?*

"This practical must-read book is for anyone who has ever suffered the
hurt and pain of mistrust. Kirshenbaum's gifted insights are profound
and they show you how to restore trust with your closest loved ones."
          —Lee Raffel, MSW, author of *I Hate Conflict!*

continued

"I Love You, But I Don't Trust You"

THE COMPLETE GUIDE TO RESTORING TRUST IN YOUR RELATIONSHIP

Mira Kirshenbaum

BERKLEY
New York

BERKLEY
An imprint of Penguin Random House LLC
penguinrandomhouse.com

Copyright © 2012 by Mira Kirshenbaum
Penguin Random House supports copyright. Copyright fuels creativity, encourages diverse voices,
promotes free speech, and creates a vibrant culture. Thank you for buying an authorized edition of
this book and for complying with copyright laws by not reproducing, scanning, or distributing any part
of it in any form without permission. You are supporting writers and allowing Penguin Random House
to continue to publish books for every reader.

BERKLEY and the BERKLEY & B colophon are registered
trademarks of Penguin Random House LLC.

Library of Congress Cataloging-in-Publication Data

Kirshenbaum, Mira.
    I love you, but I don't trust you / Mira Kirshenbaum.
        p. cm.
    ISBN 978-0-425-24531-6 (pbk.)
    1. Man-woman relationships   2. Trust.   3. Betrayal.   I. Title.
HQ801.K5657 2012
155.6'453—dc23   2011028874

Berkley trade paperback edition / February 2012

Printed in the United States of America
28th Printing

Book design by Tiffany Estreicher

While the author has made every effort to provide accurate telephone numbers and Internet addresses
at the time of publication, neither the author nor the publisher assumes any responsibility for errors,
or for changes that occur after publication. Further, the publisher does not have any control over and
does not assume any responsibility for author or third-party websites or their content.

To all of us: Because, in spite of how hurt we are,
in spite of how often we screw up, we still keep trying as best
we can to create a world where trust makes sense.

Contents

Part One

YOU *CAN* RESTORE TRUST IN YOUR RELATIONSHIPS

Finding Your Way Back to Each Other

I KNOW. YOU FEEL so hurt, so scared, so angry. There's nothing worse than when someone betrays you and you feel you can't trust them. You can't imagine it's possible that you would ever trust that person again, and at this moment you may not even want to try.

And yet . . . hope is a stubborn thing. Somewhere deep inside you, you sense a spark of possibility. Maybe, just maybe, the terrible mistrust you feel isn't the end of the relationship. Maybe trust can be restored. Maybe the relationship can heal.

Then again, maybe you're afraid that hope doesn't make sense right now. I understand. I've felt all this myself. And so have millions of other people who've been through this.

Here's what Heather told me.

Heather's story

When she got the first hint of what Chris had done, Heather was immediately swamped by those bitter, dizzy feelings of suspicion we all know so well. It's like when an earthquake starts: anything is possible, none of it good.

In a kind of manic, dread-filled daze, Heather searched through Chris's computer and checkbook. When she finally found the awful confirmation of her suspicions, she was so angry she couldn't stop shaking. She was glad he wasn't around because at that point she truly felt like killing him. It was as if Chris wasn't her husband at all anymore. He was the man who'd killed her husband. This loathsome imposter certainly wasn't the man she'd married. He was a clueless, selfish jerk.

As Heather waited for Chris to come home, the wild heat of her anger brought her to one clear decision. And so within minutes of his walking in the door she'd thrown him out of the house. His clothes, his laptop, his iPhone, and then him. "Now you can go sleep in a motel and think of some more people you can screw over, you bastard," she yelled and slammed the front door so hard a family picture fell off the wall.

Chris pounded on the door, saying he wanted to explain, that he hadn't meant to hurt her, how he was sorry. But Heather's screaming terrified him so much that he decided he'd best leave, and off he drove. As she watched the red taillights of his car disappear down the street, she thought this was the saddest sight she'd ever seen.

Friends try to help. Heather sat there as dusk turned into night. Her brain was racing, spinning dark scenarios, churning up clouds of pain that made clear thought impossible. There was a tightness in her chest, a lump in her throat. She was caught in a tug-of-war between rage and grief. It suddenly hit her: I'll never sleep again. How would she ever regain her peace of mind? If this could happen, anything could happen. Would the rest of her life be like being in an abusive relationship where you're always waiting for the next blow to fall, the next betrayal, the next disappointment?

Part of Heather wanted to get as far away from it all as she could, and that just made her feel more trapped. Because she couldn't get away. Not today anyway—not with her kids, her job, her . . . life. The sadness of it all hit her, and she started crying.

Heather called her three best friends and within an hour they were all there. As each one arrived, Heather repeated the whole story of what Chris had done and how she'd found out about it and how mad she was and how her life was ruined.

Finally, they all settled in to talk about what Heather should do.

Good, they all agreed, you threw him out. He deserved it.

But what next?

WHAT NEXT? That was the question hanging in the air. Mary said, "Look, you can't trust him, right? How can you trust him after what he did? He broke your trust into a thousand pieces. Trusting him again would just be stupid. It's all over."

"Yeah," Gail said, "I mean, this is about who you are. If you let him back, he's going to think in the end he can get away with hurting you. You can't let yourself be a doormat."

Nicole hadn't yet spoken, but Heather was starting to get the picture. Her friends wanted to see her as a strong heroine. They wanted her to show them that a woman wouldn't take crap from a guy. If she didn't take Chris back, their husbands would be that much more scared of betraying them.

Heather was heartbroken at the thought that she'd suddenly lost everything and she started to cry again. "I loved him so much and now I can't ever trust him again and I've lost everything. It's over forever."

There was a long silence, and then Nicole finally spoke: "Oh sweetie, I know how awful this is for you. I mean . . . *Chris*, for God's sake, who'd have thought he'd do something like this? And you've counted on him for everything," she said, taking Heather's hand. "I know you feel he's destroyed your world. You want to kill him. We all do. But"—and Nicole took a deep sigh—"all this it's-over-forever talk . . . I just don't know. Yeah, I know, it feels like everything's smashed into a million pieces. How can you ever trust him again? But you're saying, 'Oh, now I've found out that Chris is really this evil man.' But what if he's not an evil man? I know he loves you." Nicole squeezed Heather's hand for emphasis. "What if he's just a big, fat idiot who made this horrible, stupid mistake? What if he's really sorry and would do anything to get you back?"

"I don't want him back," Heather said.

"You don't want him back because you think you can never trust him again. And maybe that's true. I can't promise it's not true. But you still love each other and . . . *more important than that you guys had a really good relationship.*"

"For a very long time, too," Mary chimed in.

"Yeah," Nicole said, "so after you've made him suffer for a while and scared the crap out of him . . ."

"Definitely let him know you've seen a lawyer," Gail said.

". . . yeah, and scared the crap out of him, why don't you take him back and see if you can get to the point where you can ever trust him again."

"I just don't think . . ." Heather started but Nicole interrupted her.

Nicole's story

"It *can* happen. I've seen it." Nicole paused. "And I've lived it." All eyes were on Nicole now. "A year after Dave and I were married, I found out that he'd cheated on me with an old girlfriend about ten days before our wedding. I mean, this isn't what happened with you and Chris, but still, a betrayal is a betrayal. I was *so* mad and . . . *humiliated*. Of course I know how you feel. I totally felt the same way. But . . . I don't know. Something told me not to flush this relationship down the toilet. And it was hard. Really hard. I didn't trust him. My *body* didn't trust him. But I decided to give it a shot. I'm sure we made every mistake in the book trying to heal things." Nicole squeezed Heather's hand again. "But we *did* heal things. That was eight years ago, and we have two beautiful kids and Dave is a great guy and I love him and we have a good life and . . . I'm so glad I hung in there. If I hadn't, I think I would've regretted it forever."

"Do you trust him now?" Heather asked intensely.

"Do I trust him . . ." Nicole stared into the far distance. "Dave is not a perfect person. Can I say he'll never ever do anything at all to disappoint me or hurt me ever, ever again? I don't know. I do know that I've hurt *him* many times." Nicole leaned forward. "People hurt each other. The more you love someone, the easier it is to get hurt. But do I trust Dave now? I do. I trust him with my life. I can sleep at night. And during the day, I'm at peace. And about you . . . ," Nicole looked back at Heather, and said, "I'm just saying broken trust can heal. If deep down Chris is basically a good guy—and I think he is—and you have a good relationship and you love each other—and I know you do—well, I think you should give it another chance."

"I don't know," Gail said.

"I think Nicole's right," Mary said.

"So what are you going to do?" Nicole asked Heather.

"I don't know . . ."

WHO DO YOU identify with in this story? At different times in my life I've identified with each of the women in this story. I've been in Heather's position: hurt, scared, confused, blindly struggling to do whatever I could to protect myself. I've been in Gail's position: cynical, skeptical, prickly. I've been like Mary: wavering and confused.

But now I'm in Nicole's position. It's kind of surprising, actually. I would've thought that the more I saw of life, the more mistrustful I'd become. Life is supposed to make you tough and suspicious, right? But I've seen so much in my life and work that's pointed me toward the wonderful possibilities for restoring trust.

Many of us have been in Heather's shoes. Maybe it came on all at once, a shocking discovery that blasted the foundations of trust. Or maybe it crept in slowly, small acts and words that ate away at you, eroding the trust between you until you began to doubt everything you once wholeheartedly believed to be true. Either way, we've had the sickening sensation of feeling the worm of mistrust gnaw at our hearts. And once we're filled with suspicion and doubt, what do we do? Scold? Leave? Try to ignore the problem? Yell and scream? Most people in this situation report living in a state of pain and confusion. Our world has become a nightmare. We don't know what to do or where to turn. The person we perhaps care about most has become our biggest threat.

But still, Nicole's got it exactly right. Broken trust can heal more often, more completely, than most of us have ever thought. And I'll go even further than Nicole. Broken trust can heal more *quickly* than most of us have thought, too. And it's worth it, because whoever coined the expression *The broken places are stronger where they heal* is absolutely right when it comes to trust.

When bad things happen to good relationships, we no longer have to choose between a painful breakup and the pain of staying in a broken relationship. We can have our old relationship back, but made new.

Is this really possible? Oh, yeah. I've seen it over and over in my work. And in my own life, too.

My story

If you're dealing with betrayal, you're not alone. Trust issues plague people today the ways fleas plague country dogs. They've plagued me too.

I got married during my senior year of college, when I was twenty. There were many reasons for our hitching up so young, but one big reason was that he made me feel safe and I thought he was a really good guy. And it turned out that he *was* a good guy.

But he wasn't perfect.

Something happened several years later that seemed to destroy the trust I'd thought we had: My husband confessed to me that he was "involved" with another woman. He told me that they hadn't had any physical relationship, although he did admit being attracted to her. He called it an emotional affair of some sort. All I knew was that my heart was broken, the specialness of our love was destroyed, and my ability to trust him was smashed into a thousand pieces.

So I know what it's like to feel totally betrayed.

I know about the pain and the fear and the sadness and the feeling that you've almost lost your mind.

And I know the all-consuming anger.

I also know about little things, like the crazy but overpowering impulse I had to confront the other woman. One day I had the idea of going to the town where she lived and driving up and down the streets until I saw her, even though I didn't know her name or her address or what she looked like.

I know about the obsession to squeeze out of my husband every detail of their relationship, even though each of those details was a dagger in my heart, and even though I didn't believe anything he told me anyway.

I know about the intense desire I had to control him.

I know about how my world shrunk so much that the only things I did were things to make myself feel safe. Like staying angry and cold all the time.

I know about how his cheating on me made me want to go and find some guy somewhere and have a revenge affair.

I know about the shame of an uncontrolled desire to snoop through his stuff in the hope of finding some painful, damning piece of real evidence I could believe in—like a love letter to her where he laid out every disgusting thing they'd done—rather than just hear the insubstantial assurances he gave me.

I know about the feelings of rage that got so bad that I truly felt like killing him.

And I also know about this sad, terrible fact: Many of the perfectly natural, normal ways I reacted caused incredible damage to our relationship.

I was a bright young therapist then and you'd think I would have known better. But now, having worked with countless couples and individuals dealing with the pain and damage of broken trust, I realize that in dealing with my husband's betrayal I made every mistake in the book. Each one of those mistakes prolonged the pain and further damaged us as a couple. I came within inches of destroying a marriage that had been good—and is still good—*great*—now many years later. The only way I could've handled things worse would've been to shoot him.

These days, I don't judge myself for having handled things so badly. I now know that being betrayed makes everyone blind and crazy.

NEVER DID FEELING RIGHT FEEL SO BAD. It was one of the worst periods of my life. There were moments when I was convinced my heart would just shrivel up and die. And there were times when I thought the white-hot anger would engulf me in flames. I was angry at my husband, angry at the woman who would get involved with a married man, and angry at myself for being so stupid, for not being aware of what was going on, for not doing something to prevent it. Could I have prevented it? Could I have been to blame? Could I have been more attentive? Less nagging? (And there I went down the rabbit hole of self-blame—so common, so likely to make us feel even worse. Blame is never the answer.)

I hated my husband; but in those moments when I could see beyond my hatred for him, I hated myself. I hated my rage, I hated my judgmentalness, I hated my fear. And I hated how miserable I felt. I mean, why should I have felt so bad? I hadn't done anything wrong. I hadn't cheated. I hadn't lied. I hadn't acted irresponsibly. He had. He was in the wrong. He'd messed everything up, so it was his job to fix it. Right?

You may likely be feeling this way, too. But this wouldn't be a very long book—or a very good one—if all I had to say was, yeah, that person who hurt you is a no-good sack of crap and it's up to him to fix things and until he does you're damned entitled to sit there feeling mad as hell.

Sure, that was my attitude then, but if you're going to trust me, then I've got to tell you the truth. And that means I've got to report that that attitude just didn't work for me and it hasn't worked for any of the people who've come to me for help. And the thing is that on some level I knew it at the time, and I bet you do, too.

So here you are, and there I was, feeling more right than we ever have before and yet we never felt worse. Never did feeling right feel so bad. I knew there had to be a better way.

THE TRUST IMPERATIVE

Can love survive betrayal? I believe it can. I've seen it. I've lived it. Hell, if betrayal necessarily kills love, then love is too fragile to exist in the real world. Because the world is made up of imperfect people who make mistakes. Imperfect people—people we love—will too often hurt us and disappoint us and betray us, which will set up a chain reaction that too often destroys a relationship.

Well, if we can't stop ourselves from hurting the people we love and being hurt by them, then we have only one choice: We have to find a way to repair the damage that's done when there's been a betrayal.

And let's face it: There's a lot of damage. If the relationship doesn't survive . . . well, everyone always underestimates how costly breaking up is. Financially. Emotionally. The toll it takes on the kids. It may not necessarily be permanent, but it's still painful, still destructive, and it still sets you back.

But forget the damage to the relationship for a moment. Suppose the relationship survives just fine. Still, you no longer feel safe. And so you feel depressed. Anxious. Stressed. You lose sleep. There are nightmares. Rage.

And if these weren't bad enough in themselves, these consequences can have huge negative effects in our lives. They can set us back in our careers. They can damage relationships with friends and family. They can cause us to make bad decisions. And there are health effects to consider as well.

Understanding the full extent of the possible damage makes it all the more important that we know how to heal our relationships when there's been a betrayal. Because the damage just doesn't have to be so bad. Not by a long shot. You see—and this is the most important point—*it's not the betrayal by itself that causes most of the damage. It's the poor way we handle the aftermath.*

Because of our imperfect nature, because we're imperfect people in imperfect relationships who hurt each other, there will be trust issues in almost every relationship. The betrayals that haunt us aren't only the major ones. Even little leaks can eventually sink a big boat, and even small betrayals—some little lies here, some thoughtless remarks there—can create a corrosive atmosphere of mistrust.

Research shows that, depending upon how you define "trust issues," between 40 and 70 percent of couples know they have significant problems with trust. At least 90 percent of couples will have a crisis of trust at some point.

And this is where our repair work comes in. We need to restore the trust because I firmly believe that while you can't have people without betrayals, if only little ones, **you can't have love without trust.**

Having trust makes love come alive. Trust isn't just the basis for a relationship; it's the lifeblood that keeps a relationship healthy.

The biggest difference trust makes in any relationship—and not just an intimate one—is that you can relax, be open, be yourself. Just think about it: If you can't be yourself because you're not feeling safe, then even if the other person "loves you," he's really just loving a stranger, the person you're projecting who's not really you. And so how can you feel loved if it's not the real you who's being loved? And how can you keep on giving love if you're not feeling loved?

But when you trust each other so that you can be yourself and be open, the roots of love grow very strong. They grow into your very being.

You and I are designed for trust. It is woven into the fabric of our being—the need to trust others, the need to be trusted by others.

WHAT MAKES US SUCCESSFUL. Trust is rooted in our social intelligence. It's part of what makes us a successful species. We're successful not just because we're smart, but because we're smart enough to cooperate with each other. I'm not saying we're not suspicious; we are. But think about this: If we need a doctor, most of us will ask a friend for a recommendation, and we'll trust our friend to give us the name of someone good. At most, only 2 or 3 percent of us will run a background check on him. The rest of us will go with blind trust, take our clothes off, confess the most personal details, and put our lives in that stranger's hands. On the way home from that doctor, we will stop by the supermarket and buy food that we trust isn't tainted. Then we'll swing by to pick our kids up from soccer practice, and the coach who has had charge of our kids is a stranger we trust with what we prize most.

We couldn't function without trust.

IT'S ALL ABOUT TRUST. To realize how essential trust is to us, let's compare ourselves to people who are clinically paranoid. Paranoiacs are convinced that everyone is out to get them. Many have delusions about just how this is happening. The barista who makes her latte? A spy for the government. The person he works with in the office? Out to destroy him. Her sister? Sleeping with her husband. It's like being caught in a spider web: traps and danger everywhere.

You can see how exhausting and crippling mistrust is. Paranoiacs can't form the relationships that enable them to cooperate with anyone. And they exhaust themselves having to live without that cooperation.

The trust imperative is so woven into our being that there is actually a trust hormone, oxytocin, whose main function appears to give us the ability to trust. A growing number of experiments with animals and humans show that, contrary to the beliefs of many psychologists and behavioral economists, we not only have the capacity for, but a propensity for, trust across a wide variety of situations.

Trust—not mistrust—is our default mode as a species.

Just think about what you value in a relationship. Based on my research, I have found that no one really expects perfect intimacy and perfect communication with a perfect partner. We are willing to settle for an imperfect relationship with an imperfect person *as long as there's trust*. "I know that, no matter what, he's got my back," is the ultimate accolade and for many of us the ultimate satisfaction. It really is all about trust.

FINDING A WAY HOME

So here we are. I've just told you that trust is the most important element in a relationship and you're probably ready to scream . . . or cry. Because chances are, you don't have any trust left. You're hurt and angry and confused and you don't know what to do.

Back when I was going through that terrible time with my husband, what I really wanted—and what I'm betting you want now—is for someone to lead me out of the terrible place I was in. A place of confused, lonely rage. And, beneath that, bleak misery without any end in sight. But beneath *that,* the sadness of a lost child who just wants to find her way home, the way I felt as a little girl when my parents would take me to Coney Island and somehow with blinding speed I'd always manage to get utterly lost.

There's just one difference. When I was a kid and I got lost, I still had a home to go back to. But when we feel we can't trust someone anymore, we don't know if that relationship should exist for us anymore. We're anxiously wondering, What do I do? Where do I go? How do I handle all of this? Most of all, we're wondering, Can I ever trust this person again? How could I possibly regain trust? And even if I could, would I want this relationship anyway?

All these questions have answers, and it's going to be easier to find them than you might think.

I will give you everything you need to find your answers so you can see what's best for you and finally wake up from this nightmare.

I know, right now it feels impossible. Right now this feels as difficult as gluing back together a china teacup someone stomped into a thousand pieces.

But I believe I can help you restore the trust you think you've lost forever. Why do I believe this? Because over many years I have worked with people in all kinds of relationships dealing with all kinds of mistrust, and I have helped them get to a place where they could trust again.

I won't pretend I invented all the help offered here. I've learned a lot from people who'd struggled with the aftermath of betrayal on their own. They made a lot of mistakes, but they also hit on some terrific ideas. So this book isn't my telling you what to do. It's my pointing at the success of people just like you and saying, "There, do what they did and you'll come through this better than ever."

TAKING THE PATH OF TRUST

Today I'm very glad I hung in there with my husband as we stumbled our way into restoring trust. But I did it the hard way. *You don't have to.* It's not only that I've learned from my own mistakes. I'm just one person. I've also learned from the mistakes of the countless people who've shared their stories with me and those who've come to me for help.

This is the book I desperately needed when I was going through what you're going through now. I know how overwhelmed you feel. And I know how terribly conflicted you feel: You want back the trust you think you lost, but another part of you doesn't think you'll ever feel safe with this person again.

Look, I don't know if trusting the person who hurt you makes sense, but as you work through this book, if you conclude that trying to trust again is the right thing to do, I can help you get there. It's going to take some work, and I can't promise it won't be painful at times. But if you want your relationship to work—and part of you must if you're reading this book—then it is imperative that trust is restored.

HOW BROKEN TRUST HEALS

So how do we do it? How do we heal the trust? Well, let's go back to the betrayal itself for a moment. **A betrayal happens when you don't take into account another person who is relying on you.** If someone makes a date for lunch with me and then doesn't show up, I'm going to feel betrayed, if only a little. It's a betrayal because I feel that if I'd mattered to him, he wouldn't have blown me off. His not showing up means he didn't take me into account because—why else?—I didn't matter enough to him. **Anytime we treat someone as if he doesn't matter, he's going to feel some disappointment and betrayal.**

In the grand scheme of things, a missed lunch date is not such a big deal. He'll say he's sorry and maybe make amends by treating me to lunch when we do get together again. End of problem.

But suppose I'm getting married and the night before the wedding my fiancé goes out, gets drunk, and winds up having sex with my "best friend"? That is a big deal. He's *really* not taken me into account. What could I possibly mean to him for him to do something like *that*?

And that's where people are when there's been a betrayal. And there's a huge mess. First, he didn't take me into account. Then, of course, I'm furious, and even if he recognizes that that's justified, his being assaulted by my anger makes *him* feel like I'm not taking *him* into account. After all, he never meant to hurt me. It was all a big mistake, right?

THE BETTER PATH. Now we're at a fork in the road. We can turn toward dysfunction or we can turn toward healing. In the dysfunctional route, things just get worse and worse, often surprisingly quickly, and pretty soon the relationship is blown out of the water, with both partners not taking the other into account.

The restoring trust route is the opposite. Yes, it starts with the same hurt and anger. But the mechanism for healing is quite miraculous, as are all mechanisms for healing. Having done something to radically *not* take the other person into account, the trust-healing process consists of finding ways *to* radically take the other person into account.

Instead of escalating impatience, there's growing patience.

Instead of anger that goes nowhere, there's real listening and a real sense of feeling seen and heard that goes somewhere new and very important.

Instead of inflicting pain, there's an understanding of how to better meet each other's needs.

If done right, people can discover how to take each other into account in ways they've never done before. People can feel they matter to each other more than ever. The betrayer and the person who's been betrayed—even though at the beginning they may have never felt more torn apart from each other—become intimate partners in this rebuilding of trust. That's one of the reasons why when it's all over, so many people say that their relationship has never been stronger.

It can be the same for you!

2

All the Ways Mistrust
Enters Relationships

I N CHAPTER 1, I shared the story of Heather and Chris, but you may have noticed that I never said exactly what Chris did that hurt Heather so much. Maybe you assumed he'd cheated on her or wrecked her finances by playing loose and fast with their savings. But, in fact, I didn't offer any clue about what Chris had done. And that was on purpose.

As I'm going to show in a moment, there are all kinds of betrayals, more than you can imagine. Of course it matters to you which one it is in your situation because it's your life: that's what you've experienced. But, from the point of view of healing mistrust, what matters is that now you feel betrayed and you're scared and furious and are burdened with a pile of mistrust you're afraid you'll never be able to crawl out from under.

So what are all these different ways suspicion and mistrust enter our lives?

Let's get one thing out of the way. We're NOT just talking about affairs here. There are lots of ways people betray each other. And small betrayals matter a lot, too. Whether you've been eaten by a lion or been bitten by ten thousand tiny red ants, either way it's really bad. And so whether it's one big betrayal or a bunch of smaller ones, it's still all betrayal and it all destroys trust.

Trust is broken *whenever* someone we're counting on fails to live up to our expectations. When that happens, we're hurt and it feels like a betrayal.

And it feels intentional. Even if the other person swears up and down that it was just an accident, we believe that if that other person cared about us they wouldn't have had that accident. It's not just what he or she did in itself that makes it a betrayal; it's that we weren't considered a priority. And that's the key. Betrayal in any of its forms has a way of making us feel like we're nothing.

Now let's look at all the different ways disappointment, mistrust, and betrayal can affect a relationship.

MAJOR BETRAYALS

Anything upsetting and earthshaking that makes you wonder "Who *is* this other person and how can I possibly have a relationship with him?" is a major betrayal.

One woman married a guy who'd been an English major at a prestigious college and was working toward his MFA in poetry. Great, she thought. I'm marrying a smart poet. After they married, he suddenly realized he cared about money, got a job on Wall Street, and became a hedge-fund guy. This switcheroo felt like a major betrayal to her. After all, how could she trust him? She didn't even know who he was anymore.

Most major betrayals, though, are not about someone directly changing their identity. They're about someone doing something that hurts you, scares you, leaves you feeling vulnerable.

- One guy felt completely betrayed when he discovered, after they'd been intimate for three years, that his girl-friend had genital herpes. She'd known about it the entire time and when he confronted her, she claimed it was under control with medication.

- One woman couldn't talk to her mother for years after she discovered that her dead father hadn't been her biological father.

- One man found out that his wife had stumbled onto her old boyfriend on Facebook. She'd contacted him, and they went on to exchange intimate, romantic, steamy emails.

- One woman felt betrayed because her husband lent much of their life savings to his goof-off brother.

- One woman found out after ten years of marriage that her husband hadn't gone to Harvard. He'd gone to the University of Rhode Island. (Not that there's anything wrong with URI!)

- One woman found out that her sister was always saying bad things about her behind her back. She claimed she was just kidding, but it sure didn't feel like that to this woman.

- One guy married a woman who had two kids from her previous marriage. She promised him, pounding the table when she said it, that, "No, I don't want any more children," and yet before the honeymoon was over she was talking to him about wanting another kid.

- One woman had felt that her boss was a friend and mentor. Then she discovered that he'd repeatedly kept her away from opportunities for promotion because he didn't want to lose her.

- One man took his sister to the Emmys, where something he'd worked on was nominated. He was expecting his beautiful sister would do him proud by being charming to his associates. But she'd been drinking and was in a lousy mood and she was rude to the people he introduced her to.

Maybe someone's said to you, "Baby, you rock my world." Well, what all these major betrayals have in common is they rock your world too, but in a bad way. A really bad way. Someone you were counting on crapped out on you. But it's not just a disappointment; it's a breach in a fundamental expectation. I'd be disappointed if my contractor didn't finish a job on time. I'd feel betrayed if he robbed me.

With all the betrayals above, it's like going through an earthquake—which is bad enough!—in a place where you thought there weren't any earthquakes. Because a fundamental expectation has been violated, it is no longer possible for you to feel safe in your world.

BEING UNRELIABLE

Beatrice usually worked later than her husband, Tom, and brought home a bigger paycheck. It wasn't an unexpected situation; when this high-powered attorney married a school teacher, she knew what their life would look like and she was okay with it. She had married Tom because she loved him, not for his earning potential. He was kind and loving and a great father to their two kids, always there for them after school and able to shuttle them to their extracurricular activities.

But she did expect certain things. When she came home after ten or twelve hours at the office, all she asked was for him to have the kids fed, have something prepared for her to eat, and clean up the kitchen.

Too often, though—very often, actually—Tom got "distracted" and none of this got done.

One night after returning home a little later than usual, she was assaulted by dishes in the sink, an overflowing garbage pail, and the kids just sitting down to instant mac and cheese— again!—and Beatrice just lost it. She was tired, frustrated by an unreasonable client at work and had just endured a horrific commute home—and now this?

Beatrice slammed down her briefcase and screamed, "Really? Don't you think I do enough earning the money to pay our mortgage, the school tuition, and the lease on your new car? Do

I really have to come home to this, too? Sometimes I think I'd be better off as a single parent. I could hire a nanny who would take care of the kids and keep the house clean!" And with that she burst into tears, stomped off to their bedroom, and slammed the door.

When she cooled down and emerged an hour later, Tom had cleaned up and he offered a heartfelt apology. He promised, with tears in his eyes, that it would never happen again, that he would take care of the kids and the house, and she would never come home to a mess. He said that he'd write it in blood if she wanted, that from now on he was going to do it all.

And he kept to this for a couple of weeks but then he started forgetting again. They fought over this. She cried. She yelled. She felt like such a fool for making a big deal of it, and yet she really, really wanted to kill him.

So maybe your mistrust comes not from any one big thing but from a lot of little things, maybe just from an insidious pattern of unreliability.

- Your partner is always late.

- Your brother always "forgets" to check in on your parents.

- Your spouse keeps losing his job.

- Your friend keeps agreeing to do something but then . . . he doesn't do it. There's no follow-through. It's as if his promise to do it is a fraud. You feel like a sucker, and it makes it really hard for you to trust him.

Wherever it comes from, it's exhausting: this feeling that you can't count on someone whose life is woven into yours.

In some ways, unreliability can be worse than a major betrayal. It all happens gradually and you try to put up with it. So in some way you see yourself as being an accomplice: How can you blame someone for getting away with what you yourself have put up with? In a sense, you have been betrayed and have also betrayed yourself.

And when someone you depend on is chronically unreliable, that person always pleads that he can't help it, she's doing her best, it's not his fault that things work out the way they do. This inability to take responsibility is both infuriating and deeply discouraging.

BIG DIFFERENCES

Mistrust doesn't have to come about because of what the other person does. It can come from who he is. I'm talking about when there are significant differences between two people in background, personality, or preferences.

The more similar someone is to you, the more you have similar expectations and respond to things in a similar way. But when two people are very different they can get tangled up like a Sumo wrestler trying to dance the tango with a clown.

For example, if you like to plan and your partner likes to just wing it, your partner's way of doing things will seem wrong to you and you'll feel that you can't trust him.

I knew one couple where the husband was brought up in a family where the father was a distinguished surgeon and the mother was an ultra-modern interior designer. So the house he grew up in had a clean, bare Japanese look to it.

But his wife had grown up in a household filled with knick-knacks. There wasn't a single blank space in her house. There was nowhere for the eye to find rest.

When she moved into his apartment, she said she loved his Spartan style. It was clean, soothing. But then a little ornament would appear here and a memento there and some pretty little things somewhere else. And he wouldn't want to say anything because he didn't want to start a fight. But he'd seethe and eventually blow his stack and then she'd cry and he'd give in on one or two of her little knickknacks.

Slowly the clutter crept in, as did the mistrust, as if each were living with an enemy determined to undermine the other. Trust was eroded for the simple reason that they were so different.

How does this work exactly? It varies. It could be that the husband just had no idea how his wife had been brought up. So now she was just a wild card of unknowns. Maybe the husband thought that by choosing him she'd chosen his way of life. Now he was realizing that there were serious limits to her commitment. Maybe he thought she'd just lied to hook him. However it happens, it sows the seeds of mistrust.

You might think that it would take a huge difference between two people to create something as harsh as mistrust. But, as it turns out, even small differences can have large effects. The neat freak and the clutter clown can end up fighting a guerilla war.

There's nothing intentional, usually, about the ways differences between two people cause mistrust. But when relationships form, they're all about how two people connect, about the ways they are similar. Differences get swept under the rug. They seem so trivial, so easily overcome, even though late at night we may uneasily contemplate the time bomb they may turn into.

UNEQUAL POWER

There's one difference that's so important that we need to look at it separately. That's when there's a difference in power. The fact that someone is your boss, for example, means that there's a power imbalance no matter how well you get along, no matter how hard you pretend that yours is a relationship between equals.

If one person has more power, the other is relatively more helpless. It's not that mistrust is inevitable, but the risk is inevitable. My having power means almost by definition that I don't have to consult you when I plan or do something. My priorities can trump yours. You and your boss might like and respect each other. Heck, you might be friends. But she might have to institute some layoffs and maybe in spite of trying to protect your job she just can't. Trust means that two people take each other's needs into account. Power means that one of the two people doesn't have to do that.

THERE ARE LOTS of ways a power imbalance can destroy trust in a relationship.

It could be the power of money. In every couple I've ever seen where one makes or has a lot more money than the other, there's a power imbalance and a lot of room for mistrust to dig deep roots. It takes a lot of sensitivity on the part of the person with more money, and a lot of acceptance on the part of the person with less money, to prevent mistrust. How, for example, can the person with more money ever be sure that the other likes him for who he is?

Sometimes the power imbalance comes from personal power. If she is more emotionally intense and expressive than he is, or if he doesn't have the slightest qualm about going off on her, that difference will mean that one feels the other has more power and there will be mistrust.

For many relationships, all you have to do is list the power imbalances and you have an instant map to all the trust issues between the two people. Just think of a power imbalance as a risk factor for mistrust. High cholesterol doesn't guarantee that the person will have a heart attack. But if you know that a person has high cholesterol, high blood pressure, stress, and that he smokes and doesn't exercise, a doctor could make some pretty good guesses about his health. And power imbalances work the same way.

And the way it works is that the greater the power imbalance, the less likely it is that two people's interests will coincide.

Hidden People

Suppose you are in a new relationship with someone really terrific—he's interesting, fun, sexy, good looking. Now here's a nightmare scenario for you. Suppose you never know where you stand with this person. He just plays his cards too close to his chest. He's not even open enough to tell you he doesn't know where he stands on the subject of making a commitment. He keeps saying "I don't know" to your questions. He changes the subject when you try to press him a little on any personal topic.

Well, what are you supposed to think? That you're safe, just because he says you're safe?

How would you feel about a doctor who wanted to treat you without telling you the diagnosis or the name of the medicine he was prescribing?

How would you feel about a teen who hid out in her room all the time, and, when you asked whether she'd done her homework, she always just answered, "Don't worry!"

It's hard to trust someone who is hidden. We don't know where she is coming from, what she wants, what plots she's hatching. We never quite believe that there's nothing going on between her ears. They must be up to something. But what? If it was something good, why wouldn't she tell you? So it must be something to worry about.

The minute you have to ask someone, "What are you thinking?" the minute you even wonder what the other person is thinking, the seeds of mistrust have been planted in the relationship.

SUSPICIOUS PEOPLE

Maybe, you realize, it's not the other person at all. Just because you feel incredibly suspicious and mistrustful, that doesn't necessarily mean the other person has done anything to betray you.

Maybe you feel the way you do because you've been hurt in previous relationships. This was certainly true for me. I know it's true these days for many men and women. After all, with so many people marrying in their thirties rather than their twenties, there are many more opportunities for us to have been betrayed in some previous relationship before we finally settle down.

And then it may be hard to settle down at all. In fact, we can never really relax, the way it's hard to relax as a driver if you've been hit and injured by some drunk maniac coming out of nowhere. It's not that we think the person today *will* hurt us the way someone in the past hurt us. It's just that we can't help being aware that this *might* happen again.

At least in this situation we come by our mistrust honestly. We've earned it in the school of hard knocks.

Sometimes, though, we haven't earned it at all. Sometimes— lots of times actually—we're just suspicious people. Nothing really bad has happened to make us suspicious. We just are that way.

You can't call this paranoia—paranoia is way, *way* at the end of the spectrum. No, I'm just talking about the large numbers of people who are more suspicious than average. We're just wired that way. There's no point in trying to explain it away. But it means that we bring into our relationships a kind of caution, a hyper-vigilance, an expectation of being hurt that's exhausting for us and exhausting for our partners.

And the thing is that suspicion has a way of going viral. Here's Laurie. She admits she was probably a suspicious person to begin with. Then a couple of boyfriends hurt her: one dumped her out of nowhere, the other cheated on her. Now she's married to Ben. He's a great guy, but Laurie can't make her suspicions lie down and go to sleep. So she spies on Ben, grills him, doubts him, drives him crazy.

One day Ben comes home from a business trip and tells Laurie about an exciting work-related project he cooked up with his colleague Ann. Laurie acted interested, but she immediately started feeling the snakes crawling around in her head. Every nightmarish scenario you could imagine.

She couldn't contain the poison. First came the questions: "Did you spend time together in your room?" "Did you sleep with her?" "How long have you been having an affair with her?"

Ben swears up and down that nothing is going on. Laurie gets a little calmer. But now Ben sees what he's dealing with, and secretly resolves not to tell Laurie anything anymore that could get him into trouble.

Now Ben's silence will just feed the growth of Laurie's suspicions. Her suspicions will harden his silence. The poison has done its damage.

Now IF YOU add up all these different ways trust issues can enter relationships, what do you have? You have our lives as we experience them. My life, for sure. Yours too, I'm guessing. What do you think? You must have seen yourself in some of the scenarios I just laid out. Why not? You're not alone. The seeds of mistrust are all around us.

So the question is, Can the damage be healed? Usually it can. More often than you might imagine. I see real healing happen all the time, even in situations where there's been a lot of hurt and damage. But what about me? you might be wondering. What if things are too far gone in my case?

Okay, then, let's look at that possibility.

3

Is It Worth Trying to Mend This Relationship?

"I LOVE YOU, BUT I don't trust you." When Laura heard herself saying these words to her husband, Tom, she realized she faced a stark choice. Stay. Or go. This wasn't like those first days when she'd yelled and screamed and told Tom she never wanted to see him again. Then she'd been out of her mind with anger and grief. Now, she was thinking rationally and knew that she had to use her head to save her heart. She knew she had to be smart about this. A couple of her best friends had talked about decisions they'd made in the heat of the moment and later regretted.

But what *was* the smart decision?

This is such an important question. Why try to heal a relationship that's not worth healing? You need to know the answer. After all, how can a fundamentally good relationship heal if you're always wondering if you should leave?

But let's back up. Tom was a guy who went from company to company showing them how they could reduce their energy costs and become more green. On one trip he'd gotten involved in a poker game, had too much to drink, and by the end of the evening had lost more than ten thousand dollars. He was horrified by what he'd done and confessed it to Laura. This was especially bad because they were struggling to save for a down payment on their first house. To him, this felt like a horrible, hurtful blunder, a major setback, but one without any evil intent.

He had no idea Laura would take it so badly. But let's face it: In the history of the world it's almost never happened that a guy has said, "I never *meant* for this to happen," and his wife has then said, "Oh, well, then it's okay."

On the contrary. How could Laura possibly feel safe at the thought of her husband running around the country, getting drunk, and losing their money to a bunch of random idiots? That wasn't okay!

Certainly not with the memories Laura carried with her of how her dad had squandered money over and over. And how her mom had put up with so much pain.

So no wonder Laura had gone nuts for the first week or so. Then, as her anger slowly started to cool, she started wondering seriously if she could ever trust him again. These last several days had been so painful for both of them. Tom had said he would never do this again, ever, ever, ever. But what if he did do it again?

The road back to trust seemed so hard. And so the question crept in: Why bother? Why even try to heal things? Why entertain the slightest risk of going through what her mother had gone through? Why not just say "Sayonara, sucker," and be done with this?

But—and this is the question Laura brought into my office—how could she feel sure it really was right to kick him to the curb? What should she do?

KICK HIM OUT OR STAY TOGETHER? This is a place everyone gets to when there's been a breach of trust. Sometimes we get here very quickly, like when there's been a major betrayal. Sometimes it builds slowly, one disappointment at a time so that the question of kicking him out or staying together only gradually takes hold.

This can be a very scary question. It can easily seem that life on the other side of a breakup is filled with loss and insecurity. What about the kids, for example? How will this affect them? Will they blame you for ending things? And what about money? How will you live? Where will you live? And, for many of us, what about our house? You've worked so hard to make it nice, but if you break up, you'll likely have to sell it or one of you will be moving out.

Believe me, I know all about these scary questions. I've spent countless hours with women and men who've agonized over them, and I've agonized over them myself.

But here's the thing. If the stay-or-leave question won't release its grip on you, then you have to face it. So then the time to figure this out is now. And I know how to help you.

Many people at this time look to the heavens and say, please, just give me a sign whether I should stay or go. Well, here it is. I'll show you what the six signs that you should look for are.

LOOKING AT THE RELATIONSHIP

There was Laura, her heart broken, sobbing her eyes out. With a voice full of pleading, she asked me, "Can I ever trust Tom again?"

I knew this was a difficult question for her. He was on the road a lot. In his world, people drank. And there were always temptations. If he didn't gamble their money away next time, maybe he'd sleep with some road floozy.

But, I said to her, why open all this up if you wouldn't want him back anyway? Why agonize over regaining trust if, supposing you could trust again, you still wouldn't be happy with him? After all, trust is essential, but there are other reasons why marriages end.

So here's the first question for everyone who, like Laura, is looking for a sign that will point to whether it makes sense to work at rebuilding trust:

Would you want this relationship if the trust could be restored?
Of course, this is a hard question when you're blinded by rage over being betrayed. Who can see past all the mistrust?

I get it. But even though it's hard, you have to try to think about the relationship as a whole, the relationship you got into in the first place; the pre-betrayal relationship.

If there's been a major betrayal, do this: Remember the last year or the last month before you discovered that your partner had betrayed you.

If it's been about a lot of little betrayals, think about the other parts of your relationship. For example, even though your partner has had trouble keeping a job, what's your sex life been like? Can you still have fun together? Can you enjoy co-parenting?

Okay, then, now that you're a little better able to see things without the betrayal lens, ask yourself if you want *that* relationship. Maybe you weren't perfectly happy, but were you happy enough? Or were you looking for an opportunity to move on even back then before the betrayal?

You have to be honest with yourself here. You see, there's a weird psychology going on sometimes. There's something quite involving about a betrayal. Yeah, I know, plenty of times people find out their spouse has cheated (or some other kind of betrayal) and immediately dump him. But very often, we get sucked in. This is a horrible, painful humiliation, but we get focused on wanting to understand *why*. We don't want out; we want answers.

We also get focused on wanting to know that *he* knows how devastated we've been. This launches endless conversations that may be harrowing but are also more intimate than most conversations you and your partner have had together in a long time. And that intimacy can be bizarrely satisfying.

So, oddly, after the betrayal you're more in the relationship than you've been in a long time. This is a difficult perspective from which to try and remember how you felt about the relationship before the betrayal.

But just try to remember some of the things you said to yourself and to your friends. Were your eyes on the exit? Were you constantly having fantasies about what your life would be like if you weren't stuck with this person? Was there a part of you when you discovered the betrayal that felt relieved because now you had an excuse to end things?

Force yourself to answer yes or no. Remember, you're not assessing your relationship now. You're casting your mind back to how you felt about the relationship before the betrayal. And back then, were you in? Or were you wanting out?

GUIDELINE #1: **If you didn't think this was a good relationship before the betrayal, if you weren't wanting to be in it beforehand, then why in the world would you want to stay in it now? But if the relationship was a good one (putting the betrayal aside for a moment, although of course that's hard), why wouldn't you want to try to salvage it?** *Most people who leave a relationship right after the betrayal have regrets if the relationship had been good before that point.*

I asked Laura about all this and she went quiet for a long time. "Honestly," she said, "I was happy. That's why this was such a shock. It had never occurred to me that we wouldn't be happy forever. I feel like such a fool that I didn't see the signs that this was coming—I've always known he was a little irresponsible—but I really did think everything in our relationship was okay."

But sometimes I get a very different answer from people.

Anne

"I think I've spent years being distracted by the whole trust thing," Anne said to me. "I was his second wife and he had four kids from his previous marriage. His first wife had died. He was pretty rich—compared to me, anyway—and very stingy. He kept saying he wanted his kids to be taken care of. But I didn't trust him, mostly because he was so powerful and would often abuse that power by bossing everyone around—me included. He was just a tough guy with a lot of money, and he pretty much just wanted to get his own way. But sometimes he could be really sweet, and sometimes he'd take me on these expensive trips. He just kept reeling me in.

"But," Anne continued, as she stared far into the distance, "I missed the big thing. I couldn't see it. And that was that we had nothing in common. I mean, we could be polite and get along with each other. And then my polite self would get upset that I felt I couldn't trust him with money. But actually I was thinking, how do I get out of this? I felt trapped. And then right at the point when I would be ready to say something, he'd take me on another trip. It was like he knew when to reel me back in."

This is a good example of someone for whom mistrust is an opportunity to leave. Who knows if Anne could've worked out her reason for mistrust (her husband's abuse of power)? But these were distractions from something more fundamental that had already been bothering her, the fact that they had little in common.

That's what you need to think about here. Is this the opportunity you've been looking for, not because of the mistrust but because of the problems that are already in the relationship?

If so, you've already answered your own question. The mistrust is a distraction. You've already decided that you want to leave.

Spoilage

Let's talk about a big betrayal. Okay, it happened. But now suppose that you had an absolute guarantee: God himself said that the other person would never do this again. Bang, you're safe. You have absolutely nothing to fear.

But does that make everything okay for you? For many of us it doesn't. Even if you're totally safe and even if he is very, very sorry, that still might not make it okay.

Maggie and Freddie

"That's what was so confusing," Maggie said. "Freddie was so sorry. He was crying all the time. And he knew, he really knew, how much he'd hurt me. Honestly, if you were to ask me to bet money, I'd bet everything that he would never hurt me again. In fact, I was pretty convinced that Freddie would do everything in the world to spend his life making it up to me."

"Wow," I said. "That sounds pretty good."

"Yeah. I mean, I think it was as good as it gets from a husband who'd done what he did. But here's the thing: I just didn't care. I wanted to care, but I didn't. It was like . . . I don't know . . . like you drop an M & M on the kitchen floor and you pick it right up again and you blow on it and it feels totally fine to eat it. The five-second rule and everything. But if you drop a piece of broiled fish on the floor, the same floor, totally clean, there's no way you're going to eat that fish now. It's totally disgusting to you. The M & M was fine, but the fish, forget about it.

"Freddie was like that piece of fish," Maggie said. "The fact that he'd slept with that woman—I mean, I could totally forgive him, that wasn't a problem—but it was like he'd fallen on the floor and you couldn't pay me to have anything more to do with him. Now here's the thing. Stupid me. It took me two years to figure this out. I got all caught up in the 'he's sorry and I'm forgiving him' business. Two years to figure out that I'm not going to eat a piece of fish that fell on the floor."

Lots of people feel the way Maggie did. There's something about betrayal that's so fundamental that, *for some people*, it seems as though the very molecules in the person who's hurt them have changed, just the way the piece of fish that fell on the floor became a new kind of thing for Maggie.

And so the question is:

Does the fact that this betrayal happened ruin everything for you?

Now you have to be careful. Please, I'm begging you to be careful. It's one thing to say, "I'm so mad at you I don't want to have anything more to do with you ever again." And anger like that can last a surprisingly long time. Months. But that kind of anger eventually goes away. When relationships truly heal, anger mostly evaporates.

But I'm not talking about anger here. I'm talking about something that goes much deeper. It's a complete re-envisioning of who the other person really is, a falling into a different category of being, the way Freddie became for Maggie.

And if that's happened for you, you've gotten your answer. You can't stay.

GUIDELINE #2: If the betrayal has changed who the other person is for you so thoroughly that you can't imagine wanting to be with him—not even after your anger has died down, not even if you knew for sure he'd never betray you again—then trust isn't the issue and you'll be better off ending the relationship.

Now this is a huge decision, of course. Even though you might have gotten the clarity you need already, you may still want to feel more certain. That's perfectly understandable.

Well, as luck would have it I wrote *the* book on this subject. It's called *Too Good to Leave, Too Bad to Stay: A Step-by-Step Guide to Help You Decide Whether to Stay in or Get out of Your Relationship*. I wrote this book for everyone who's caught in a state of relationship ambivalence. And if that's you, you'll benefit from it.

But let me put my arm around your shoulder and give you a piece of advice: If you're clear about what you want to do now, fine. But if not, give your relationship a chance. Give healing a chance. The very *best* way to see if it makes sense to stay in a relationship is to try to make it better and then decide. And then luck is in your favor. Broken trust can heal. Even when it feels most impossible.

FORGIVENESS

Okay, so maybe you now know that you do want the relationship if the broken trust can heal. But *can* the broken trust heal? Sure, I've said that in general broken trust can heal more often and more easily than most people think. But what about you? Is this true in your case?

That's what we're going to figure out next. Does it make sense for you to put yourself through the process of trying to rebuild trust?

Part of the answer to this has to do with you. Part of it has to do with the other person. Let's start with you.

I know: Everyone wants to forgive. But do you *really* want to?

Well, what is forgiveness anyway? I think for most of us, forgiveness is a feeling in the heart. It's a kind of softening and opening. Instead of our heart being hardened by anger and fear, it relaxes.

For example, if you were walking down a busy street and someone seemed to deliberately walk into you, you might be angry. But suppose that at the very moment when you were about to give this person a piece of your mind you noticed that he was carrying a white cane. Oh, he's blind! you realize. And your heart melts. Your anger is gone. It's okay now.

And that's usually why we forgive. We have some realization or come to some understanding that makes it possible for us to say, I can let this go.

The understanding doesn't have to come from realizing that it wasn't the other person's fault. It can come from you. You might just realize that your anger is hurting you more than helping you. And then you see that you don't need it anymore and you let it go. That's another way of finding forgiveness.*

Now here's what you need to know. The amount of anger you feel right now—even if it's big as a mountain—is no guide to whether or not you can forgive one day.

Jim and Debbie

Jim was furious, and deeply hurt, when he discovered that Debbie, his wife, had been holding out on him. He'd been working so hard and was so stressed over money. This had gone on for a few years. Then through a casual remark that Debbie made, he discovered that her parents had a lot more money than he'd thought. And she had a trust fund. When he demanded an explanation, she said she'd been trying to protect herself from feeling that he'd married her for her money. "But we've been married for six years!" he shouted. "For six years I've been struggling and worrying and you just watched it. Was this funny to you, with all the money you had?"

Jim needed to get away to think. This was so hard for him to wrap his mind around.

There was a part of him that thought, so what? He'd never expected his wife would be rich. He'd never expected that he wouldn't have to work hard. So wasn't this in a way good news? At least maybe he wouldn't have to worry about squirreling away money for the kids' college education.

* I have a lot of helpful insights on how to forgive in my book *Everything Happens for a Reason: Finding the True Meaning of the Events of Our Lives*, in the chapter entitled "Tying Balloons to a Stone."

But there was that nagging question: What kind of person does what Debbie did? What kind of person watches her husband struggle the way he did and could easily help but doesn't? he wondered. It was as if she had a caring deficit.

And that's how he saw her for days and days. She'd suddenly become a cold monster to him.

And then he had his big realization. That question—what kind of person does this?—showed him the way. She'd had a huge burden, too. From her point of view, if he'd known about her money she wouldn't have felt he loved her for herself. And that's what she needed—to feel loved. Every minute he'd spent working so hard and worrying about paying the bills so they could have a good life was a minute she felt that he truly cared for her.

This understanding changed everything for Jim. Debbie wasn't a pitiless user. She was just a person who desperately wanted to feel loved. Jim was still angry, but with this shift in perspective he knew he would be able to forgive her.

So this is what you have to ask yourself:

Can I imagine the possibility of forgiveness?

Can I see the other person in a way that will let me move on from what happened? Can I better understand his motives? Can I better understand what he was having to deal with? Can I better appreciate his limitations?

Then there's the way you see yourself. Can you see yourself ever reaching the point where you'd say, "This is ridiculous. I'm destroying my own chance at happiness and peace of mind because of my stubborn refusal to forgive."

That's probably the number one reason why people do forgive: They realize their lack of forgiveness is destroying their own lives.

GUIDELINE #3: If you can see your lack of forgiveness as a self-destructive act, if you can see forgiving as a life-affirming act, and if you can sense the realistic possibility that one day you might be able to forgive, it makes sense to work at healing this relationship. Otherwise, not.

TRUE CARING

Callie and Alec

Callie had been married for eight years to a man who was driving her crazy. Alec pretty much never kept his promises. He'd say he'd be home by a certain time but then he'd come home whenever. He'd say he'd set up the plans for their vacation and then he'd just not do it. When she would get upset, Alec would act very sorry and he'd promise, sometimes with tears in his eyes, that he wouldn't screw up next time.

Then one day it hit her. Out of nowhere came the realization that she'd fallen for an illusion. Alec acted sorry and made promises only to manage her. To prevent her from boiling over. He didn't care at all about how much she suffered. He only cared about how much she made him suffer.

This realization that Alec was quite happy keeping Callie on the brink of madness as long as she didn't go over the edge and make life too difficult for him, showed her that repairing her broken trust was impossible. He really didn't care if she trusted him. He just wanted her not to make a fuss every time he disappointed her.

Can you recognize yourself in Callie's story? Ask yourself this question:

Does the person you mistrust care about how you feel?
If not, why bother trying to restore the trust? You see, it's that caring about how you feel that's the key. That's their motivation.

GUIDELINE #4: **If the other person doesn't care about how you feel in the sense that he consistently hasn't gone out of his way to do things to show his caring, then he will not be able to work with you during the trust-restoring process, and so it's not likely to happen. Why bother trying?**

I'm not saying that someone who cares about how you feel will necessarily change to the point where he earns your trust. Sometimes caring isn't enough. But I am saying that without your partner caring about how you feel, rebuilding trust is impossible. With caring, anything is possible.

WORKING ON THE RELATIONSHIP

Rebuilding trust is something two people do together. You just can't say, "You go off and become trustworthy and then come back and we'll see." It doesn't work that way.

You're needing to talk to each other, to share information about what things mean to you. You've got to talk about things that are difficult to say and difficult to hear and do so without making each other miserable. You've got to share hurt feelings without creating more hurt feelings. You've got to listen when you're itching to make yourself heard and make yourself heard when you're tired of talking.

Zoe and Phil

Phil was so nice and amiable, but he just wasn't interested in dealing with Zoe. Phil loved relationships and he loved his relationship with Zoe, but he wanted the relationship to be trouble-free.

This was as confusing as hell for Zoe. Phil seemed like such a relationship-y kind of person. He liked to cuddle and hang out. He was quite happy to talk with her about any problems she was having at work or with a friend.

But if Zoe ever wanted to talk to Phil about a problem she was having with *him*, it was like an iron gate came rolling down.

There was the famous time she tried to talk to him about why he wasn't more affectionate. It actually hadn't been that big a deal for Zoe. She almost hadn't said anything. But then she did, and the more she talked, the more remote and even angry Phil seemed to become. It was as if her talking about needing more affection drove all possibility of affection right out of him.

People like Phil are often afraid of being judged or of feeling inadequate. Relationship problems somehow press all their buttons. It's a huge danger zone for them.

So when Zoe found out that Phil was in big, big trouble

because he'd been cheating on his taxes, she knew that the two of them were in big, big trouble, too.

And that's the way it played out. If he'd been hiding this from her, Zoe thought, what else was he hiding? If he'd put them in so much jeopardy with this, what else had he done to put them in jeopardy?

Zoe was angry and scared. She believed that a wife shouldn't abandon her husband in a time of trouble, but she felt she couldn't trust him and she needed his help to find her way back to him.

This was help Phil couldn't give. He was too scared, he felt too vulnerable, he was too shut down.

He'd say things like, "Look, I know I fucked up big time, but I've learned my lesson and I'll never screw up like that again. You're just going to have to trust me. And if you can't trust me, that's your problem and you're going to have to deal with it."

Phil was basically giving Zoe an ultimatum: Shut up or get out. There was no way she could shut up. So Zoe felt she had no choice but to get out.

So ask yourself this:

Can the other person work on your relationship with you?

Zoe and Phil are a clear case of when one person neither wants to nor is able to work on the relationship to heal the trust. But, please, I beg you: Don't confuse this with someone who merely has difficulty talking about relationship issues. If having difficulty talking about relationship issues meant not healing broken trust, very few relationships would heal. But so many do heal.

MAKING IT EASIER TO WORK ON THE RELATIONSHIP. Let me help you figure out whether the other person can work on the relationship. There are two main reasons why people are afraid of talking about their relationship.

One is that they are afraid of being attacked. This makes sense. Who wants to be stuck on a spit and roasted over an open fire?

But you can solve this problem easily. Don't attack. Don't blame. Don't call each other names. Yes, I know, that's just what you want to do. You're really mad! But think about what will happen if you indulge yourself too freely in that. The other person will think, "Oy, who needs this?" He'll associate talking with you with being yelled at, and so he won't want to talk with you.

So this is your choice: You can yell and call names and maybe feel a lot better in the short run but totally turn him off to the idea of talking with you. Or you can focus on making him feel what *you're* wanting to feel when *you* talk: safe.

It's just a question of what you want more. To get things off your chest? Or to keep alive the possibility of a real dialogue?

The other reason people are afraid of talking about their relationship is they don't feel that they're going to get a chance to talk themselves. Too often, "We need to talk" is code for "*I* need to talk." And what is it that we do when we talk like this? We put our needs on the table. We share our feelings. We define our reality.

Well, what's going to happen if the other person feels he just has to sit there and listen to all of that? He's going to feel there's no room for his feelings, his needs, his reality. He's going to feel squeezed out.

So why would he bother participating in this? To win a merit badge for being the super-best listener ever? If you're going to find your way back to each other, you'll have to reward him for listening to you by listening to him.

I know what you might be thinking: Wait a minute! Look at what he did to me! He damned well better listen to me!

Well, you know, it's true: having been hurt, you do have a moral edge. You do deserve more time to talk. Instead of just 50 percent of the time, maybe you have a right to 60 percent of the time, or even 70 percent. But not *all* of the time. He needs to feel he can talk, too.

GUIDELINE #5: **A good way to tell if the other person is willing and able to work on the relationship is this. What happens if you attack less and listen more? If that makes the other person more willing to work on things with you, then you're in good shape. If it doesn't make a difference, or if you can't bring yourself to attack less and listen more, then you may not be able to go through the process of rebuilding trust.**

By the way, if you went into couples therapy to deal with the betrayal, you'd end up spending good money to have someone get you to attack less and listen more, even though you're the aggrieved party. What did you think? That you'd go into therapy and have free rein to attack and talk without the other person being able to get a word in edgewise? So why not do it right on your own and save the money?

Why Not Give It a Try?

Joey and Cathy

As it turned out, Joey and Cathy didn't lose their house. But they came very close. For years, Joey's gambling problem had made their lives miserable. It took Cathy a long time to catch on. It always seemed as though there was no money, but Joey, who was in charge of their finances, would always talk about how expensive things were or how he'd missed out on a bonus.

Still, Cathy couldn't shake the sense that something was not right. Then one day Joey came home looking as if he'd been in a bad fight, and the headlights of his car were smashed in.

Joey confessed the whole thing: the money he'd lost gambling. His constant attempts to catch up and get back to even. The shady loans he'd taken out. How he'd fallen still further behind.

Cathy's trust was gone. It wasn't just this unbelievable horror of how he had thrown his family's money away, putting all of them into a deep hole. It was how she knew he was in the grip of a terribly destructive illness.

But Joey begged her to not give up on him. He got down on his knees, the way he had when he'd asked her to marry him, and pleaded with her to give him a chance to earn back her trust.

"Why should I trust you, Joey?" she said. Joey surprised her. He promised he would go to Gamblers Anonymous meetings every night of the week. He said she could take him if she wanted. She could sit there with him if she wanted.

And he would give her complete control over the family's finances, such as they were.

And that's when a strange thought floated into Cathy's mind. "Why not? What do I have to lose?"

Clearly they'd already lost all of their money. Nothing would be easier, or make more sense, than leaving him. But it changed everything for her when she realized that the cost of staying was minimal. *You can always leave. But once you leave, working things out stops being an option.*

Cathy thought about her regrets. Right now she had a lot of them. All the money they'd lost. The peace of mind that was gone. But if she was going to end her marriage and lose that, too, she wanted to make sure she wouldn't regret that decision.

And what would be the one thing that would make her regret leaving? Joey kicking his habit. What if she left and it turned out that she'd bailed just when better times were coming?

Besides, she could always bail later.

She told him, "Joey, as long as you go to meetings and stop gambling I'm going to give you a chance to earn my trust back. I don't expect you to be a perfect person, but there's no reason you can't go to those meetings every night. You just promised me that. So forget the past. But I'm trusting you to keep that promise now. If you do that, we have a future. If you don't, we're over."

It was the best decision Cathy had ever made. Joey did keep going to meetings. He did manage to avoid gambling.

So that's what you have to ask yourself:

What do I have to lose by giving our relationship a chance?
What you're really asking here is, What will it cost me if I'm wrong? It's not about locking yourself into a lifetime commit-

ment. It would have been a mistake for Cathy to commit herself to an entire lifetime with a compulsive gambler (or anyone who's betrayed her trust). But that's not what she was doing. She was just making a commitment to a process. She made it clear to Joey that if the process broke down, they were history. Cathy's idea was brilliant. Yes, when trust is broken it's devastating. Yes, a lifetime of mistrust is impossible. But for all the damage that's been done, the cost of trying to rebuild trust can be surprisingly low.

Think about it. What's the worst that can happen? The person who's betrayed you will show that he hasn't changed. He's still meeting his supposedly ex-lover. He still keeps forgetting to do all the things he said he was going to do. He places another bet on a sporting event.

Okay then. Now you know. He can't—or won't—do what he needs to do to deserve your trust. Think of it as his way of letting you go. And now you can go, free from the possibility that you'll regret not having given trust a chance.

But it could also work out. If you do it right, and if he wants to earn your trust, it will work out.

And then you'll be glad you gave it a shot.

GUIDELINE #6: If you can get to the point where you can say you have nothing to lose by giving the other person a chance, then it's worth staying and working to rebuild trust.

These six questions and guidelines should have given you the clarity you were looking for. But if you have any doubt at all, if you're feeling at all iffy about the decision to leave, I very much hope you will give love and your relationship another chance. Try to rebuild trust. The process works. And once you find that trust can be restored, the other person will look very different to you.

4

Yes, You Can Trust Again ... Success Stories

STILL READING? GOOD! It means you think there is just a chance things can be salvaged—and that they're worth salvaging. You might be full of doubt at this point. Most people are. And you're probably still angry and sad. But that's okay, too. Right now you don't need more than the wisp of a feeling that it just might be worth trying to restore trust.

I know about whatever doubts you might be having at this point. You're afraid that once your trust has been broken, you can never get it back. If someone you care about has betrayed you, you think, things will never be good even if the other person is perfect forever, and who can be perfect forever?

Or even if you think trust can somehow be rebuilt, you think it will take forever. I remember one guy who was deeply hurt by something his wife did and he said to her, "You know when I'll be able to trust you again? When you're on your death-bed and I've seen that between now and then you've done nothing else to hurt me." His wound was very raw at that point, and that's the kind of thing people say when their wounds are raw.

And even if you think that trust can be rebuilt and that maybe it won't take forever, the process of restoring trust seems completely mysterious to you. You have no idea how to make it happen. And that sense of utter helplessness makes you feel discouraged.

So, rebuild trust? they say. *Why bother? It's too hard to rebuild trust, and who can do it anyway?*

BROKEN TRUST CAN HEAL

For some of us, it doesn't make sense to hope that trust can be reborn any more than it makes sense to believe that dead bodies can come back to life. And why should it? We've all seen relationships destroyed by mistrust. The destruction seems to have a momentum of its own, the way you know that if a house is engulfed in flames it will soon collapse in a heap of charred timbers.

But *is* that what broken trust in a relationship is like?

No. What's burned is burned, but what's broken can heal. And broken trust in a relationship is not like a house on fire.

It's like a broken arm. Broken arms heal all the time. Yes, it's painful. And, yes, it can feel like it's taking forever. But it doesn't take forever at all.

Broken trust can heal. I've seen it happen over and over again. Here are some examples.

Stacy and Ed

They had been married for about a year when Stacy discovered that Ed had been talking to his ex on the phone. He denied that he had feelings for her, claiming that she was just a good friend. Ed had broken up with his ex when he found out she was cheating on him. But before that, things had been pretty passionate between them. Stacy had gotten involved with Ed on the rebound and had always felt very insecure as far as his ex was concerned. Now she was afraid that his ex was trying to get him back, and she felt horribly betrayed. Ed saw how hurt Stacy was and promised that he'd never again talk to his ex. But Stacy thought, "What's the point? Maybe I'll say, oh, I trust him again, but I'll never be able to get back to that place where I knew I could trust him without having to think about it."

Ed might have hurt Stacy by staying in touch with his ex, but here's the thing: Ed and Stacy's love was real. Nothing can destroy real love between two good people in a good relationship. And Stacy found, as they worked through their trust issues, that their love was as strong as ever. In fact, in the end she realized she loved him more because she was impressed by his willingness to work to regain her trust. And Ed loved Stacy more because he saw her capacity to forgive.

I know I've left out how they got to this better place. That's what the rest of this book is for. And I know this sounds like a fairy tale at this point. But it's real and I've seen it work out this way countless times.

Maria and Sean

When Sean learned that Maria had lied about her age, he was furious. Sean was thirty when they met and Maria told him that she was twenty-seven. Somehow that seemed just right to him, part of all the other things about Maria that seemed just right.

But a couple of years after they were married, they went to get passports, and that's when he learned that Maria was five years *older* than he was. Sean was furious. All he could think was that Maria had just been trying to trap him. She'd wanted to bag a husband. What other lies were there that he hadn't uncovered yet?

Maria cried and begged him to forgive her. But it felt to both of them as though nothing could ever make Sean's anger go away. Wouldn't he always feel their marriage was just a trap?

But Maria hung in there and accepted his anger, even though it was very hard. Eventually Sean came to understand the insecurities that had driven Maria to lie. How she was driven by fear of losing this man that she'd fallen so much in love with. Slowly, imperceptibly his anger melted. And he was able to see what a basically honest person Maria was. His broken trust healed completely.

Tanya and Keith

A few years ago, Tanya and Keith got into a terrible fight over her in-laws. Tanya had wanted Keith to stand up to his parents so they wouldn't keep interfering with their lives. But Keith felt caught in the middle. Tanya got frustrated and started saying things to Keith like, "Be a man. Stand up for yourself." At one point Keith felt so belittled that he grabbed Tanya, shook her, and roughly pushed her away. She went right into the wall.

Keith's act of violence made Tanya feel that she could never trust him again. She said to me, "Look, maybe I can get to the point where I can pretend that everything is okay, but he hurt me very badly, more emotionally than physically. If he can do that once, he can do that again. I'll never feel safe with him."

BUT THAT WASN'T TRUE. Neither Tanya nor Keith had a clue about the amazing power trust has to heal. And here's what happened. Keith got help and was able to show her that he'd learned and changed. And Tanya came to believe that. Tanya got help, too, to deal with her anger that had precipitated their fight. The trust that had been damaged got returned better than ever.

WHY YOU CAN BELIEVE THAT TRUST WILL BE RESTORED

These are not once-in-a-lifetime stories. Stories like these happen every day to people like me and you. Beyond this evidence, there are other reasons for having hope that trust can be restored.

One of these reasons is that the person who's broken your trust is very possibly not as bad as he seems to be right now. People are wonderfully complicated and have all kinds of unexpected depths. People can disappoint you—you know that already. But those same people can also be filled with surprises that move you.

One woman was convinced her husband was a lazy bastard

with a bad attitude. But was he? No; one day he got a job he cared about that made him happy and he turned into a hard-working guy who seemed a lot sunnier.

One guy found out that over the years his wife had cheated on him with two different men. There was a huge blow-up that almost ended their marriage. But was she completely untrust-worthy? No. There were issues in their relationship that needed to be worked out, and before long she promised that she would never cheat again, and she didn't. I know that because I was their therapist.

ONE TRUTH. There are lots of reasons to believe that trust will be restored, but let's look at this one.

When we've been betrayed, we think we've discovered the truth about someone. But in fact all we've done is discover *one* truth about them. We've discovered that they can do this bad thing. Fine. Now we know. And, of course, it's devastating.

But where does that leave us? Knowing this bad truth about someone doesn't mean that no good truth about them is possi-ble. Not at all. The person who betrayed us might well turn out to be someone who is genuinely sorry and has a real capacity for regaining our trust.

I know what you're thinking. But they did that bad thing! Doesn't that say something?

I understand. We all think that when we discover that some-one's done something bad, it reveals his true character.

But, besides being a bad person, there are lots of reasons why someone might do something that might turn out to be hurtful.

Maybe he had no idea what effect it would have on you.

Maybe she somehow just fell asleep at the switch.

Maybe he was just carried away by the impulse of a moment. Maybe she didn't understand what she was getting into.

You can't let a bad thing that someone has done blind you to their good qualities. We're all capable of doing things out of stupidity, weakness, ignorance, or selfishness. But the most important thing about us—about you and me and the entire human race—is that our good qualities can redeem our mistakes.

And it's so easy to overlook someone's good qualities.

Sara and Tom

Remember the woman I just mentioned who was convinced her husband was a lazy bastard with a bad mood? That was Sara. She had completely forgotten that her husband, Tom, hadn't always been this way. In fact, he'd been a sunny, hardworking guy when they met. This is a mistake we all make: to assume that now is forever. When I get a cold, for example, it bums me out because I think I'm going to stay sick forever. My coughing and sneezing is my new eternal reality.

And so when we've been betrayed we think that this new piece of bad behavior will last forever. And sometimes it does. But lots of times it doesn't. Lots of times there's a reason for the bad behavior, and when the reason goes away, so does the bad behavior. Sara had the luck or good sense to hang in there long enough for Tom's situation to change and then he changed too.

HOPE IS NOT A PRECONDITION. Sara stuck it out without any great hope. And that's *really* important for you to understand. Hope is not a precondition for accomplishing important things. We often make a mistake about hope. It's almost as if we think hope is a gift we have to bring to something worthwhile, the way you might bring a bottle of wine or a box of chocolates when you go visit someone. But it can be the opposite. Instead of hope being what you bring to launch the right action, hope can be the gift the right action brings to you. Hope can be the way you find out that you've done the right thing.

So right now you don't need to have hope that you two can rebuild trust in your relationship. You just need to think that it's worth attempting, if only so you can say that you attempted it.

Life is full of surprises. And many of the very best surprises start after we've lost hope.

Anyway, one huge reason to give rebuilding trust a chance is this possibility that the other person can surprise you with their good qualities as they've just surprised you with their bad ones.

Rebecca

Let me tell you about a woman who took a huge leap of faith and how it paid off for her.

Rebecca came to me because she'd heard that I do a lot of work with people who are trying to figure out if they want to stay in their relationship or leave it. She was pretty sure, however, that she wanted to leave. That was because she'd caught her husband, Daniel, cheating on her.

Rebecca was a very busy lawyer who worked long hours. Daniel was a musician and composer who mostly set his own hours. He'd often spend a lot of time at home feeling lonely, missing Rebecca. It was that loneliness that lead him into a relationship with a young woman he was giving guitar lessons to. Once a week she'd come to their house, get her guitar lesson, and then they'd go on from there, if you know what I mean. Rebecca came home early from work one day because she wasn't feeling well and found Daniel in bed with this woman.

How do you get over a betrayal like that?

I asked Rebecca to bring Daniel with her the next time she came to see me. I soon learned a lot. Daniel was very sorry, I discovered. Heartbroken, actually. And he was rather naïve. It was a giant newsflash for him that Rebecca would be so totally devastated by his cheating. Of course he understood her being upset. But he'd thought that when your wife finds out that you've been cheating, she yells and screams for a while, makes you sleep on the couch for a few nights, and then the whole thing blows over. He was completely unprepared for the idea that Rebecca would experience his cheating like the murder of a loved one.

I also found out that they'd had a great relationship. They really enjoyed being with each other. Sex was great. They shared a passion for nature and music and Latin dancing. Of course, this is part of why Rebecca was so devastated. How could Daniel have thrown away something so good?

But, I pointed out, Daniel may have cheated, and that was horrible, but he wasn't the one throwing away their relationship. He'd made a gigantic mistake, but now he wanted to heal things. He wanted to fight for their marriage. Rebecca was the one who was talking about throwing it away.

The fact was, they were already rebuilding the trust that had gotten broken. Daniel was learning how and why Rebecca was so devastated. She was getting to learn what had driven him to cheat. Sure, things still felt awful, but the trust-restoring process had begun.

Still, Rebecca felt stuck. With all this communication and understanding that was beginning, she couldn't be sure she could trust him ever again.

And that's when a crazy idea came into her head. They each had one child from a previous marriage. Daniel had been adamant about not wanting any more kids. But Rebecca wanted another child and time was running out. It occurred to her that if he would agree to have a child with her—not because he wanted to but because he knew that it was important to her—that would make a huge difference. And she would know that she really mattered to him.

"But why would you want to bring a child into the world whose father didn't want it?" I asked.

"Oh, you don't know Daniel," Rebecca said. "If we have a child, he'll love it and be a wonderful dad."

And when she heard herself say these words, something went through her like a jolt of lightning. Finally she was able to reconnect to her memory of Daniel the good guy, not Daniel the bad guy.

So she said to him, "I can't make any promises, but if you agree to have a child with me, because it means so much to me, then I think my rage and hurt will heal a lot faster."

Daniel had a lot of qualms and questions. But that was okay. This was a big deal. And before long he said okay, and Rebecca knew he meant it.

I recently heard from them. The baby who'd been just an idea in their heads is about to start kindergarten. Daniel is a good dad. Their relationship is good again. And Rebecca has come back to trusting him.

STILL MORE REASONS
WHY HOPE MAKES SENSE

There are still more reasons why it makes sense to be hopeful that trust can be rebuilt. One of these reasons is the power of goodness, which we so easily forget.

We're all so hungry for good things to happen, and a good deed can be powerful. We've all seen TV commercials where a single paper towel wipes up a big spill. Well, that's the way it is with goodness. Trust can be restored because the people wanting to be trusted again will so often do something so wonderfully good that it moves the relationship to a whole new level.

We actually just saw this in action with Rebecca and Daniel. His willingness to have another child to make Rebecca happy and as a way of making amends was an act of goodness that changed (or restored!) who he was in her eyes. He went from being the kind of guy who does bad things to being the kind of guy who does good things.

But you don't have to have a baby to fix things, thank goodness! One woman decided to trust her husband again for the simple reason that as she poured her heart out week after week, telling him over and over about all the ways he'd hurt her, he just listened, without complaining. It was hard for him to be raked over the coals for such a long time, but still he gave her the gift of listening until she'd said all she had to say.

We may not see these good things right away. The dynamic usually goes something like this. We're hurt and we get angry. The other person is apologetic but often gets angry, too. It's only a little later in the process that people usually find their way to doing something good. But when that happens, it can be transformative and provide a powerful reason to have hope.

And, as you'll see, if you can avoid most of the mistakes that almost everyone makes after a betrayal, trust will be restored much faster.

A KIND OF WISE FOOLISHNESS. No matter how badly hurt we are, there's a part of us that can't and won't accept the death of a relationship. It once was good. It may have been very good up until the moment you discovered that you'd been betrayed. Well, many of us are not psychologically wired to immediately turn around and say it's over now.

This isn't foolishness; this is wisdom. There's a part of us that understands something, even though we too often forget it. It's that **nothing is as wonderful as it seems at its best, and nothing is as terrible as it seems at its worst.** So although we do get carried away by hope and disappointment, there's a part of us that knows we shouldn't.

There's always time to leave when you've discovered that in your particular case the mistrust can't heal. And there are plenty of situations, as you'll see, where you can realize that the betrayal broke something that was already damaged. Not every person, not every relationship can recover from a betrayal. I totally get that.

But if you're caught up in the anger and despair that comes from being betrayed, you need to know that you'll never lose the option to leave. You just have to be on the lookout for the possibility that staying makes sense, and it makes sense more often than people think in the heat and pain of the moment.

THE NATURAL TRUST-RESTORING PROCESS

Finally, there's what may be the most important reason of all for why hope makes sense: the process a relationship *naturally* goes through when there's been a betrayal is a *healing* process if nothing interferes with it.

In fact, by nature we are designed to be trust-building creatures. The intensely social life of human beings is no accident. Physically weak and slow compared to all the animals our ancestors hunted, we could only survive if we worked together. And we could only work together if we trusted one another. People without a basic capacity to trust and to earn trust tended to die out.

As we moved from being a hunter-gatherer people to being an agricultural people, trust mattered even more because cooperation mattered even more. The rise of capitalism would have been impossible without the willingness to trust and without the ability to earn trust.

Think about it like this: Every friendship you have, every relationship you have that's worth anything, came about because of your taking a chance on trusting someone. Of course there's a part of us that's wary and suspicious. But we also know that not trusting, in the end, is a one-way ticket to loneliness and isolation. And none of us wants that.

It's our trust-building nature that's a big part of the reason we find betrayal so horrifying. It's not just that we don't feel safe, as awful as that is. It's that the betrayal and the mistrust that follows feel like a crime against nature. Life is not supposed to be like this, we think.

That's why, if we can muster any kind of hope and energy, we'll pick ourselves up, dust ourselves off, and try in the best way we know to restore trust.

Sure, the process is painful, but if you do it right it can be much less so. And sure, it often seems to go wrong. But actually it's the mistakes we make along the way that cause all the trouble. If you know

- what those mistakes are

- why you make them

- how to avoid them

- what to do differently that really does work

your broken trust will heal, as has happened for so many others.

5

The Secret of Restoring Trust

IT'S A PUZZLEMENT. We want to trust. We *need* to trust. We're designed by nature to be trusting creatures. The process of healing trust is perfectly natural. And yet we screw it up over and over again. What is the mysterious source of these disastrous failures to heal broken trust?

And what if these failures, once they were properly understood, could be easily prevented?

As you know, it's not the things we don't know that hurt us the most. It's the things we think we know that are actually wrong that cause the real damage. And it happens all the time, not just when it comes to healing broken trust.

A hundred and fifty years ago, women giving birth in hospitals died in great numbers. This was an awful situation, and a lot of people thought that some huge, dark force must be responsible for it. As it turned out, there was one hospital in Vienna that was dedicated solely to childbirth. It was staffed only by mid-wives. And here the death rate was far, far lower.

What was the difference between this hospital and all the others? It was, a Dr. Semmelweis noticed, that there were no sick people, no accident victims, no cadavers. And in those days, before people understood that germs existed, doctors didn't wash their hands between patients. Semmelweis figured that there must be a connection between women dying and doctors touching sick people or cadavers before assisting in a childbirth, because the deaths weren't happening in the childbirth-only hospital.

So Semmelweis went on a campaign to get doctors in his hospital to wash their hands before touching a woman in labor. There was incredible resistance at first. But eventually they tried his idea, and the death rate plummeted, first at his hospital and eventually around the world. Childbirth in hospitals became safe and, by the way, our understanding of germs took a huge leap forward.

What a terrible problem: so many women dying in child-birth. What a simple, stupid mistake: not washing your hands. What an easy solution: hand washing.

Once upon a time, the birth of a baby was made safe by avoiding one simple mistake. Today the rebirth of trust is some-thing that we can look forward to if we just know what mistakes to avoid.

But what is it that we mistakenly think that we're doing right when it comes to healing broken trust?

TRUST VS. SAFETY

Oh, those crazy snakes that crawl through our head when we've been betrayed. Honestly, I'm getting upset just thinking about what I was like in those weeks after I first learned that my husband had been having that affair. I really was like a crazy lady. It felt as if I was surrounded by enemies on all sides. That's the weird thing about mistrust. When you've been seriously betrayed, the whole world feels shaky and treacherous.

Our thinking goes something like this: If *he* could hurt me the way he did, then *anything* can go wrong, *everything* has the potential to blow up in my face. I can't even trust *myself.*

And that's when the trouble begins. The healing of broken trust is a natural process. Trust itself is natural. So why do we get so bent out of shape that we actually do things to *prevent* trust from healing?

THE BATTLE WITHIN. I work this way. All my friends work this way. All my patients work this way. Honestly, I don't know anyone who doesn't work this way.

And you probably work this way, too.

There are two parts of us. There's a trust-hungry part, and there's a betrayal-vulnerable part. And the trust-hungry part guides us easily and automatically unless the betrayal-vulnerable part is aroused.

Because we want to trust, because we were designed by nature to function best in an atmosphere of trust, trust is our default mode. If we don't have a reason *not* to trust, then we *will* trust.

And even if there's been a betrayal, we still want to trust. Our desire and need to trust, is so strong that we will trust again—surprisingly quickly—unless we're confronted with a reason not to. And this is where our betrayal-vulnerable part comes in. If anything happens that even slightly can be perceived as an offense, the betrayal-vulnerable part of us will be stimulated and rear its ugly head, wreaking all sorts of havoc.

Let's go back to the broken arm analogy. When we break our arm, we put a cast on it. The arm wants to heal, and it will heal unless we wiggle it around or someone bangs into it, so we protect it.

For trust to heal quickly and easily, nothing should stimulate the betrayal-vulnerable part of us. We need to protect it. Sounds like a plan!

Unfortunately, people aren't perfect. Not you. Not the person who's hurt you. Even if the person who's hurt you is so sorry he can't stand it, his imperfections will lead him to do things that will jostle your betrayal-vulnerable part and scare you. He might get mad. He might forget to call you. And since you've been so furious, he's become quite intimidated, so he might avoid telling you something that he knows will get you upset. And when you find out about it, you might get even more upset.

Under normal conditions, missteps like these are no big deal. But remember: We are betrayal-vulnerable. These minor incidents stimulate our mistrust.

And we're not perfect either. Oh boy, are we imperfect. We respond to a peacemaking overture with anger and disgust. We spurn his attempt to understand how we feel. We push him away when he tries to make a healing gesture. These mistakes slow down the healing process, if they don't sabotage it completely.

They may be very common and quite understandable—and believe me, I do understand—but they're destructive because they slow down or prevent the healing process.

Let's take a glimpse at how this plays out in action.

Cindy and Jeff

Cindy is a middle-aged woman with many accomplishments, and is embarking on a brand-new career. She's quite bright and beautiful. With her wild curly let-all-the-gray-hang-out hair and her peasant-style clothes, she's what Boston people call a "Cambridge type."

Her husband, Jeff, is a thin, hip, and grizzled-looking writer with a worldwide reputation, someone who would look equally in place at a West Village cocktail party or on a cracker barrel in front of a country store.

Cindy is feeling terribly betrayed. No, Jeff didn't cheat on her. He announced that he bought a cabin on a lake in Maine where he wants to go and spend time writing. It was to be a kind of personal home away from his home, far from any distraction. "Don't take it personally," he said. Ha! How could she do anything *but* take it personally? She didn't see this as a new writer's shack that just happened to be far away. She saw this as a trial separation that he was throwing at her out of nowhere.

She told me that if he'd cheated with every woman in the world she wouldn't have felt more pushed aside.

She is hurt, scared, furious, devastated. Nothing about her world makes sense anymore. She's still the same person she always was. Better. But now Jeff doesn't want her. She thinks of all their favorite restaurants, but now she can't look forward to going to any of them with him. She remembers all the good times they've shared and becomes bitter because "How can he throw it all away?" In fact, even when Jeff tries to do something nice for her she sees it as a sign of his betrayal. Even a little compliment, once so welcome, now seems like a man placating a woman he's cast aside.

And in her hurt and pain and fear, she unloads wild machine-gun volleys of rage. Sometimes she switches to a sniper rifle as she tries to hit him with the most wounding comments she can think of, such as, "You're so interested in making me feel like shit because you realize what a mediocre writer you really are, something pretty much everyone else has figured out already." She attacks; sometimes he cowers, and sometimes he attacks back.

It's all unbelievably sad, because they are two people who had relied on each other and loved each other and built a good life together. They can see how they're slowly ripping their wounded marriage to shreds, but they don't know what else to do.

Jeff has blamed the whole thing on his needing to give his writing a shot in the arm.

Cindy says that explanation isn't good enough.

This poor couple sat before me, completely torn apart. Jeff looked at me with tears in his eyes and said, "What else can I say?"

I looked at Cindy for the answers, but of course she doesn't know. How could she? All you know in a situation like this is that you can't trust someone you love and rely on. Or is it "used to love and used to rely on"?

And it feels like torture. It's the pain of an emotional wound that hasn't healed yet. If you stub your toe, you know the pain will go away before long. The pain of betrayal feels like it's going to stay around forever, because the betrayal itself seems like it's destroyed your world. You can never change the fact that it happened, so why would you think the pain could lessen or morph?

When you've been betrayed, it feels as if you've been stranded on a tiny barren desert island. You might figure out how to survive but it will never feel right.

And when you're in pain like that, you lash out. And so Cindy lashed out. It was perfectly understandable. I had done the same. We all have.

Is Mistrust a Fatal Relationship Disease?

Suppose, just suppose, that the things we do in our emotional pain are . . . how shall I put it? *We could do better.* Yes, they're understandable from an emotional standpoint, but from the point of view of restoring trust, they're not so smart. In fact, they're mistakes. It's like scratching away at chicken pox. Understandable, yes. Smart, not so much.

Look at what happened with Jeff and Cindy.

The real reason they came to work with me wasn't really because of Jeff's decision to get a cabin for himself. It was all about the aftermath, the disturbing way their anger kept boiling over and didn't subside. It was disturbing for Jeff, because, like all people who've deeply hurt the person they care about, he was hoping Cindy would get over it fast. As for Cindy, she was disturbed because the longer she stayed angry, the more it made sense to her that they should end their marriage. Why stay married to someone when you're that angry with him and it's that hard to get over it?

They were falling into the trap where the longer it takes to restore trust, the more anger there is. And the more anger there is, the harder it is to restore trust and the less reason there seems to be to stay in the relationship. *That's* why so many of us have the experience that mistrust is a fatal relationship disease.

But it isn't. **Mistrust can heal—it's the anger that prevents it from healing.**

I know what you're going to say. Cindy said the same thing. *Aren't I entitled to be angry?*

Well, sure. Of course you are. Believe me, I'm the last person in the world to tell you you're not entitled to your anger. If someone hurts or disappoints you, of course you're going to be angry. Sometimes our anger is the best sign that we're strong and alive and able to take care of ourselves. In fact, as you'll see, anger can be a healthy part of the trust-restoring process.

The problem comes when anger takes on a life of its own. Anger is like the Wicked Witch in *The Wizard of Oz*. She has her role to play, and she's entitled to it. The movie wouldn't be the same without her. But the movie is not about her. She's not supposed to triumph or take over the movie. Otherwise, poor Dorothy. Poor us!

UNDER ATTACK. Jeff, as you can well imagine, was someone who totally hated it when anyone was angry with him. Most people do. The other person's anger is their jail, and they want to be let out! When someone's really mad at you for a long time, it feels like an endless nightmare of punishment. And it never feels reasonable because, of course, we focus on our intentions, which were almost always good, whereas the person we hurt doesn't care about our intentions, not at the beginning anyway; she only cares about what we did.

At one point Jeff said, "But where does all this anger come from?" It was a good question. Sometimes I'm surprised there isn't even more anger. Look, as I said to Jeff and Cindy, it's not just that someone has done something to hurt you, although they have; it's not as if someone stepped on your toe and your toe hurts. It goes much deeper. Betrayal feels like a devastating and humiliating attack—even if it's a relatively small betrayal.

Let's say Joe forgets Sally's birthday. It's not that big a deal in the grand scheme of things; it's not like he lost their life savings in a gambling binge. But it's not nothing either. Of course Sally's going to be furious. It's not just that Sally had to spend all day waiting for Joe to surprise her and then ended up with nothing, like an idiot. It's also humiliating, because what is she going to say when everyone asks her what Joe got her for her birthday?

Joe is going to say he forgot, that he never meant to hurt her. And he probably didn't, but what good does that do? Sally is going to feel that Joe is saying "My life is far more important than yours. You don't matter. I do." And that's deeply hurtful.

Well, if it's like that when someone forgets a birthday, which people do all the time (memo to my husband: no, this does not give you an excuse for forgetting my birthday!), think of how much worse it is when someone really does betray you. They've destroyed your past and your hopes for the future. And they've destroyed your peace of mind in the present in ways that you never would have imagined.

With Cindy and Jeff, there was all this anger and it wasn't

going away, so she felt they really needed help. How in the world could she and Jeff figure out a way to prevent her natural and understandable anger from destroying their relationship?

We have to understand what's at the root of this anger. Just think about it. When you've been betrayed, whether it's one big thing or a bunch of little things, you're going to be feeling this terrible sense that you're just not safe in your world. And that's a big deal, because we have no greater need than to feel safe. It's programmed into us by Mother Nature. When you look at any animal, what you see are all the characteristics that make them safe. The zebra's stripes, which camouflage it, and its ability to run fast. The squirrel's side-facing eyes, which make it possible for it to see danger, as well as its ability to run up a tree in the blink of an eye. The porcupine's quills. The bee's sting.

Safety, for an animal—and for us—is everything. We can't go along in our lives without feeling safe.

And that gets at the heart of how trust issues can go on to destroy relationships.

Look at what happens when someone disappoints or betrays us in some way. To take a small example, let's say you said you'd show up at my house at 7:30 for dinner. But you didn't arrive until 8:30, and you didn't call either.

Now my trust is damaged. *And because I can't trust you, I don't feel safe.* If you could hurt me this way, who knows what other ways you could hurt me? If you were an hour late for our dinner appointment, would you show up in time to take me to the airport? Would you show up to help me move? Would you be available to support me if something bad happened in my life?

Now if I were a saint, I'd immediately try to figure out how we can reestablish trust between us. But I'm just a poor old sinner like everyone else, swept up in not feeling safe, and so my focus is going to be on doing something to make myself feel safer. It may not be a smart thing to do, and it may not work, but when we're scared we act on impulse.

For example, I may yell: "I'm fed up with your coming over late, especially when you don't call and don't answer my texts!" Often yelling *does* make people feel safer. What better way to let the other person know, *fast*, that this is a big deal for me? What better way to scare the other person? Once I've yelled, I feel better, stronger. Because I feel safer.

But the tragedy and the trap is that the things we do to make us feel safe won't restore trust. They just damage the relationship instead of healing it.

IT'S WHAT CATS DO. When you feel betrayed, you feel incredibly disempowered. Helpless. There was someone you thought you could count on, and in some way he let you down. That makes you feel that this person could do things to hurt you and there's not much you could do about it. How do you prevent someone from lying to you? How do you prevent someone from not doing what he said he was going to do? How do you prevent someone from cheating on you? You feel powerless.

The only way we can feel safe at a time like this is to make ourselves seem as powerful as possible. Fiercely powerful. Terrifyingly powerful.

It's what cats do. When my cat sees a threat—usually imaginary in his safe little world—he turns sideways and bristles up all his fur and starts hissing, making himself look and sound as big and scary as he can.

People do that, too. We yell, threaten, attack. We hope that if we scare the crap out of the person who betrayed us, he will be too scared to ever betray us again. *That's* why the person who's been betrayed has so much anger. It's naïve to say that we're angry because "This is just how I feel." We're angry because it's a response given to us by nature to make us do things so we'll feel safe.

Believe me, when we get upset because someone's hurt us, at that moment we have a lot more in common with a cat than a philosopher.

And in fact focusing on safety *works*, if our only goal is to put up a wall that we can live behind. Hey, if you were going to have a meeting with someone you find intimidating, you could wear a suit of armor! If you never want to be hurt by anyone, don't let anyone into your life. It's impossible to betray a hermit.

And that's the problem: *Focusing on safety completely back-fires if our goal is to restore trust and repair the relationship.* The things we do to feel safe usually damage relationships. Anger creates more anger. Distance breeds more distance. Just think about every really horrible fight you've gotten into. One of you says or does something terrible. The other does something even more horrible. And then things escalate until it's a total disaster. But each of those horrible things is an act of aggression designed to make the person saying it feel safer. And in the end, we're safe but alone. All we've done is get in the way of the healing process.

Think about something as seemingly simple as making a new friend. At the beginning you don't have a relationship. You're just two strangers. If your safety needs are paramount, you won't have anything to do with this person. Why would you? This person could turn out to be a maniac or a con artist, so you keep your distance and keep safe.

But if you sniff out the possibility of a relationship, and are open to that possibility, you have to trust. Your desire for a relationship has to trump your need for safety. At a minimum, you'll start sharing some information like your name and what you do for a living. You'll probably talk about some personal things, too. It's amazing what we can learn about a stranger from a casual conversation. But that's only possible when we put our relationship needs ahead of our safety needs. Sometimes we get hurt. But most of the time it's worth it.

THE UNROMANTIC CAVEMAN. A very good question might have crept into your brain by this point. How could nature have allowed something so dysfunctional as focusing on safety over trust to evolve?

A long time ago, when we'd barely stopped dragging our knuckles on the ground and all this stuff was evolving, life was all about survival and survival was far from certain. Men and women probably formed monogamous relationships, but they were more businesslike. They were for the purpose of having children and making a living. No romantic expectations there among the cavemen!

And people died at a much younger age. Women died in childbirth. Men were eaten by tigers. People were done in by fevers.

With short lives and low expectations, the cost of focusing on your safety needs was much lower. Life was very much about safety anyway. So it's not that nature allowed a focus on safety to evolve; the safety focus was already there, going all the way back to our lizard ancestors.

It's trust that was the new thing. As I suggested earlier, our brains and our ability to communicate complicated information evolved, and people were able to cooperate to do things our ape ancestors never dreamed of. The benefits of cooperation were gigantic. They led to agriculture and cities and writing and technology and to the whole trust-based world we live in today. Without cooperation, we couldn't have our world. Without trust, we wouldn't have cooperation.

So when we fall back on our safety needs, we're falling back on responses that evolved in a very different world from the one we live in now.

SLEEPING IN A NAZI'S BED

Okay, so now you can see why it's been so hard for you and me and everybody else to heal broken trust. It's not that broken trust is hard to heal in itself. It's that the things we do to make ourselves feel safe when we're living with mistrust prevent the broken trust from healing.

In other words—and this is very good news—broken trust is hard to heal because we're not even trying to heal it. We're just trying to make ourselves feel safe.

As these words echo in my head, I think about my growing-up years, which were very much a school for mistrust. We were Holocaust survivors, displaced persons, refugees. If my mother was able to keep me and my brother alive during the chaos of postwar Europe, believe me, it wasn't because she was a simple, trusting soul. She was as suspicious and focused on primitive safety as they come.

I probably would've become just like her. But let me tell you a story about how I ended up sleeping in a Nazi's bed. This was one of the events that showed me the possibility that trust makes sense, that trust is essential.

THE MAN ON THE TRAIN. I was seventeen, which is how many years the war had been over. And there I was, a blonde, blue-eyed American Jew, traveling by myself through Europe after my first year in college, sitting in a compartment of a German train headed toward Munich.

Sitting opposite me was a German man telling me something I'd heard a lot as I traveled through Germany. How he'd been just a poor, dumb soldier during the war. How he'd known nothing about the murder of six million Jews, to say nothing of the millions of others killed by the Nazis. How he was very sorry for what had happened, but even if he'd known what was going on he wouldn't have been able to do anything about it.

But I didn't believe a word he was saying. I'd heard his spiel too many times. No one had known anything. No one was responsible. Some people had gone so far as to say that nothing had even happened.

I told the man that I was a Jew and that with all due respect I didn't believe him. Hitler had been very explicit about his program. The round-up of Jews had been very public. Soldiers had brought back stories of atrocities. How could anyone not have known?

The man got upset. It wasn't from guilt. It was from my being so rude as to spoil his convenient little narrative.

"You don't know what it was like during the war," he said

angrily, and then he proceeded to tell me. The more he talked, the angrier he got. And the angrier he got, the more he sounded like a Nazi. In the movies, the Nazis always sounded angry.

I asked him if he'd been a Nazi. "Of course," he said belligerently. "I had no choice. Everyone was expected to join."

A woman I took to be his wife started rolling her eyes. The whole thing made her uncomfortable. I was making them remember something they wanted to forget.

But I wanted to remember. This, in a way, was a homecoming for me. I was on my way to a town outside of Munich called Leipheim, where there'd been a displaced person's camp after the war. I'd lived there from the time I was six months old until four years old. It had been a former German army barracks.

So I'd lived where Nazis had slept before and, as you'll see, I was going to do so again.

...AND THEN I FAINTED. I got off the train at Leipheim and so did the couple. And that's when it happened. I'd been feeling woozy on the train and somehow as I was saying good-bye to them, I fainted. I must have come to immediately, because there I was lying on the platform. The woman wanted to know what was wrong. I said I was just tired and I'd forgotten to eat for a long time. I stood up and promptly fell down again. They asked if I wanted to go to the hospital. I said no. That's when the man said, "Then you have to come home with us." It was a command, not an invitation.

I was too weak and dizzy to argue. But I was very scared. I could've said no, but where would I have slept? I didn't feel strong enough to even search for a hotel.

That was a turning point in my life. Clearly they'd both been Nazis. My head was filled with visions from old newsreels showing Germans waving and cheering at Hitler with hysterical enthusiasm. Why would these people have been any different? And now they were taking me into their home where they could even kill me, if they wanted.

But I decided to trust them. It's not as if I had no choice. I could have gone to a hospital. I could have gotten a sandwich and hung around the train station until I felt better.

But it just felt clear to me that some unknown combination of guilt, responsibility, and caring made them want to help me. Yes, maybe they had plans to kill me, but probably not.

I was stunned at my own impulse to trust them. If you had asked me if I would ever do something like that in a million years, I would've said no.

But I said yes, and it changed my life.

FILLING ME UP. They took me home. And the woman, good German housewife that she was, brought me soup and sausages and bread and tea with honey and apple strudel and everything she could think of to fill me up.

The man, perhaps because he couldn't think of anything better to do, or perhaps because he thought it would reassure me, showed me pictures of himself during the war in a German soldier's uniform, with his buddies, their arms around each other's shoulders, grinning, trying to look brave, but mostly looking tired. Oddly, they did reassure me. He was just a guy who had been swept up in the war like everybody else.

I was going to thank them and leave when I started to feel

sick again. The woman put her cool hand on my forehead and pronounced that I had a fever. "You must stay the night," she said, "I'll make a bed for you on the couch."

Soon they went to sleep, and there I was, weak and still scared, but less so. As I was dealing with my amazement at having trusted them, it hit me that *they* were trusting *me*. Okay, sure, maybe they would come in the middle of the night to kill me, but maybe they were thinking that I could get up in the middle of the night and kill them. There, only a few feet away was their knife-filled kitchen. After all, it wasn't impossible that a vengeful Jewish teenager would worm her way into Nazis' houses and commit murder.

Morning came and no one was dead, which put us all in a good mood. Plus, I'd fully recovered from whatever it was that had made me sick. I still remember the amazing breakfast the woman made. Eggs, ham, freshly baked bread, a huge steaming cup of coffee. More apple strudel. The sun streamed through the kitchen window. Trust had worked. It gave me a memory, and it gave me hope.

Mistrust had been my school. And mistrust would certainly have been the easiest road for all of us the previous night. But that night had shown me that trust can work and when it does it has amazing healing qualities.

Without that night I'm not sure my marriage would've survived after I found out that my husband was involved with another woman. Even though I'd had so many lessons in how trust was foolish, just this one experience in how trust made sense made it possible for me to believe that there could be redemption for my husband and our relationship.

And I learned something else. This couple had been taught to hate Jews, and I'd grown up hating Nazis. In fact, I'd spent much of my teen years fantasizing about being in the resistance and killing Nazis left and right. If the couple had been afraid that I'd had murder on my mind, they wouldn't have been far wrong. But just the way there's another side to mistrust, there's another side to hatred. We only need a chance to get there.

REBUILD TRUST AND FEEL SAFE

All of this leaves us with a big question. Where do we go from here if we've been betrayed? After all, we do need to feel safe. So how do we rebuild trust *and* feel safe at the same time? It sounds almost impossible.

And yet people do it every day.

Shortly after one of my daughters got her driver's license, she got into an accident. It was snowing. Because she was careless and inexperienced, she was driving too fast and skidded into an embankment, almost totaling the car. Afterward, all I could think about was how scared I was. No one was hurt, but she could have died. Other people could have died. I didn't feel safe and I didn't trust her.

I didn't want her to ever drive again. I certainly didn't ever want her to drive as long as she was still so young. Maybe we could try again in eight or nine years . . .

But things don't work that way. She needed to get back on the road, and part of me understood that. But what should I do? How should I handle it?

I didn't realize it at the time but I was in the classic safety-versus-trust dilemma. The only way I could feel perfectly safe was to never let her drive again. But here's what gradually dawned on me: The only way I could come to trust her again was if I *did* let her drive. Paradoxically, I had to feel less safe, at least in the short run, if I wanted to feel more trust.

That's what trust *is*. It's not just a feeling. *Trust is what you do when you relinquish your need to feel safe.*

For example, let's say I'm going to a restaurant I've never been to before. If I didn't feel safe about how clean that restaurant was, I'd be stupid *not* to inspect the kitchen and check to make sure all the board of health inspection certificates were up to date. Most of us don't do this, of course. And the reason is we trust the restaurant enough to relinquish our need to feel safe. It isn't trust unless you relinquish your need for safety.

It works the same way with relationships affected by hurt and betrayal.

SOLID TRUST. All hope for the rebirth of trust, for the survival of your most cherished relationships, depends on your seeing that **you can only regain trust if you let go of some of your need for safety.** You may have to do this in tiny steps. You may only be able to let go of your need for safety very slowly. And I will help you figure all this out in detail. But the secret of restoring trust—solid trust, trust that won't keep you awake at night worrying—is figuring out a way to take some risks and carefully, slowly, focus less on safety. It can be more than a little scary. But it's the only way. Let me show you.

Melissa

It's a good thing Melissa doesn't have a murderous bone in her body. Otherwise she could have killed James many times over.

She certainly had many murderous thoughts. And who could blame her? The jerk had broken their engagement three times. He'd also broken up with her a number of times before they got engaged the first time.

It was confusing and maddening. Why didn't Melissa just dump the blithering idiot? Well, he was actually a funny, loving guy, and aside from the times when she wanted to kill him, they had a good relationship. The problem was that before he met Melissa, James had had his heart broken by three women. Out of nowhere, each one had either dumped him or betrayed him. He just couldn't trust that Melissa wouldn't do the same.

Besides, Melissa was different from the other women he'd been with. They'd all been sweet, accommodating creatures. (Until they stabbed him in the back, that is.) But Melissa gave him a run for his money. She wouldn't take any crap. He loved the challenge but he was also intimidated by her intensity.

And so every now and then, when they hit a rough patch or when James was feeling particularly insecure, he'd start complaining that this was all too confusing for him, too upsetting, and that he needed more time. It wasn't really a breakup. It wasn't that they were on a break. He just wanted to put any forward motion on hold for a while.

The last time he pulled this stunt Melissa went into a real crisis. It suddenly hit her that this wasn't a game he was playing. Maybe he just didn't want her. How could she trust a man who let her go so easily and so often? Melissa couldn't trust him at all.

Since Melissa couldn't trust him, she didn't feel safe. And, of course, safety comes into play whenever we're willing to throw our relationship needs overboard to take care of our personal needs. Or, as Melissa put it, "Screw you."

She let him know that she was through with his nonsense. No more apologies, she said. No more begging to get back together. The only way she wanted to hear from him was if he showed up on her doorstep with a wedding ring and a justice of the peace.

SAFETY'S LONELY VICTORIES. Her girlfriends applauded Melissa's tough stance. It was a victory for safety. But safety's victories can be lonely. They can also backfire. Some people thought James was pulling stunts, but he was sincerely insecure. Melissa's pulling back the way she did only stimulated his worst fears: that she didn't want to marry *him*; she just wanted to *get married*. So he in turn retreated even further.

And that's what happens, of course, when people do things to feel safe. It becomes a vicious cycle: The things I do to make myself feel safe make my husband feel unsafe, and then he does things to feel safe that make me feel still more unsafe. Just think about every really horrible fight you've gotten into. One of you says or does something horrible. The other does something even more horrible. And then things escalate until it's a total disaster. But each of those horrible things is an act of aggression designed to make the person saying it feel safer.

But if someone could be brave enough—trusting enough—to break the cycle, then reversing the pattern doesn't seem quite as impossible. James kept sending Melissa emails saying he was sorry about what he'd done but also saying that he didn't want to marry her at knifepoint. Melissa got mad, but the more she thought about it, the more she saw that he was right, damn him. If James did exactly what she wanted and showed up on her doorstep with a wedding ring, what kind of a marriage would that be?

A forced marriage, that's what. He would never know if she loved him. She would never know if he loved her. All this would represent is a temporary victory in a power struggle that could very well go on forever.

So, by some kind of miracle, Melissa decided on a completely different approach. What if—scary thought!—she acted as if she trusted him? What if she said, "Look, I know you're scared. So I'm going to trust what you've said all along, that you really do love me, and that you really do want us to get married. And I feel the same way. So forget the ultimatum. If you can tell me you're ready, that will be great. And I'll wait for you to do what you need to do to get to the point where you can commit. The only thing is—and I'm just being honest here—I can't wait forever. This isn't a threat or an ultimatum. It's just a fact that I'm thirty-three and as you know, I can't wait forever to start a family."

It wasn't as if Melissa was throwing her need for safety out the window. She *couldn't* wait for James forever. It would be too humiliating, and she could end up never having a family. But she could take care of her legitimate safety need easily: just give *herself*—not him—a deadline. In the meantime, though, all she could do was trust that he really wanted to marry her in spite of the fact that he'd broken up with her many times.

It worked. Beautifully. When James saw that she trusted him, he felt he trusted her. Maybe she really did want him and not just marriage! The pressure was off, but he felt a real sense of responsibility towards her. Within six months, they went to Barbados to have a lovely beachside wedding and honeymoon.

And here's the thing. *Trusting James could not have failed.* Oh, sure, it might have turned out that James's cold feet would prevent him from moving forward with the relationship. But then Melissa would have known the truth: that when he had the chance to step up to the plate, he didn't want to do it. At least that would have been his choice. And that would have been far better than pressuring him into a marriage he didn't really want or scaring him away from a marriage he did.

After having been so often betrayed by James not wanting to commit to her, Melissa found her way to solid trust.

TRUST AND SAFETY

You might think—and you'd be wrong!—that I'm saying we have to forgo our need for safety to build solid trust. But I'm not saying that. Not at all.

First, we can't. If you discover that your husband has betrayed you and you throw all his clothes out of the bedroom window and lock him out of the house, that's not a deeply thought-out strategic move. That's an honest emotional impulse, something anyone can understand. At a moment like that, we are desperately needing to do something to make ourselves feel safe, and those needs have to be respected.

And some of the things we do to make ourselves feel safe are actually a good idea. I mean, come on: If you've been treated badly, it's not a horrible idea to do something to make the other person scared to treat you badly again. This is why we get all stern and huffy in a restaurant when we call the manager over because something's gone wrong with the way we've been treated. That's a betrayal, too, and we want the manager to know he'd better not let it happen again.

But the thing is we don't *just* want to get our jollies by yelling at the manager. We also want the problem to be made right. What's more, if this is a place we expect to keep coming back to, we want to have a nice, warm, friendly relationship with the manager. It's more pleasant, and more productive.

That's why we all have to balance our need for safety with our need for trust. And, as you'll see, that's what the trust-restoring process will give you if you can avoid making some key mistakes.

FIX IT? OR FORGET IT?

When we feel hurt and betrayed, there's always a part of us that wonders why bother working on the relationship? We're angry and discouraged and we don't trust the other person, so we have to wonder if staying makes sense. We're afraid that if we stay it will be like throwing good money after bad.

Feelings like this are normal. But you need to know: Your discouragement is *not* a sign that the relationship can't be fixed. It's just a sign of how hurt you are, and that's a big difference.

The best way to tell if staying makes sense—the gold standard—is to go through the trust-restoring process that I will be sharing with you next. Then you'll know for sure, one way or the other.

Part Two

RESTORING
TRUST AFTER A
MAJOR BETRAYAL

6

No, You're Not Crazy

THIS IS A book about healing broken trust, and mistrust can come from lots of different places—from your partner's bumbling unreliability to the ways you've been hurt in previous relationships. But when you talk to people about broken trust, the first thing that usually comes into their head is infidelity and other major betrayals.

You might be surprised to hear that major betrayals are very common. In a survey I did of more than 250 people ranging from ages 22 to 55, over *90 percent* had experienced a major betrayal in a significant relationship.

To illustrate, I recently did a workshop and asked a large room full of men and women how many of them had been betrayed. Everyone raised their hand except one guy.

"So you've never been betrayed?" I asked him.

"No," he said, "but I've betrayed someone."

And there you have it.

Betrayal is all too common but it's not because we're bad people. It's because we're limited, flawed people living with a lot of stress. Things just fall by the wayside. Sometimes those "things" are people we care about. So what exactly do I mean by "a major betrayal"?

It's a major betrayal when someone does something that breaks a fundamental promise or violates a fundamental expectation and does so in a way that significantly hurts your peace of mind.

Suppose I borrow five dollars from you and promise to pay you back tomorrow. But tomorrow comes and I forget and I don't bring you the money. It's annoying, sure. You might think I'm a jerk. You might decide to never lend me five bucks again. But in the grand scheme of things, so what? It's easier to assume that I forgot and just let it go than to make a big deal of it.

But suppose I tell your brand-new boyfriend about how you used to be really fat and slept around because you didn't feel good about yourself. And suppose you were really hoping this relationship would work.

This is a major betrayal. It's not just that I've said something about you behind your back that you didn't want told that way, or told at all. It's that I've interfered with the course of your life. I've possibly hurt your chance at love. And then you'll not only have lost a lover but a friend as well, and maybe even the possibility of trusting other friends in the future. In a strange but very real way, by what I've done I've damaged your entire world.

That's a major betrayal.

THEY COME IN MANY VARIETIES. By the way, sexual infidelity is just one of many kinds of major betrayals. Hitting your spouse is a major betrayal. Going behind your spouse's back and loaning a big chunk of your savings to your irresponsible, no-good brother is a major betrayal. Getting married with your new bride thinking you're rich and powerful when in fact you're nothing of the sort is a major betrayal. Suddenly being unavailable to your best friend when she gets cancer is a major betrayal.

It doesn't even have to be intentional. Becoming an alcoholic or losing your business or home or becoming obese are often experienced as a major betrayal even though these things are not done on purpose. Saying "I didn't intend it," even if that's totally true, doesn't make it any less a major betrayal. It's still a breach of a fundamental promise or a violation of a fundamental expectation and it still does so in a way that significantly hurts the other person's peace of mind.

If something is a big deal to you, if it changes the way you see the other person, if it makes you feel unsafe, if the quality of your life suddenly goes downhill, then it's a major betrayal.

WHAT IS TRUST? All right then, so what is trust? Trust is a feeling based on a fact. Most of the time, it's not even a feeling we're aware of. I'm sure that you trust that the chair you're sitting in right now is not going to collapse under you. But I'm also sure that doesn't give you some big, wonderful feeling of well-being. Most of the time the feeling of trust is barely more than the absence of anxiety.

Except when we've been hurt. Then the very sense of safety we used to take for granted is now something we ache for. If you manage to retrieve that sense of safety, it can feel very real indeed. Suppose you had a chair collapse under you and had it fixed so you knew that it was sturdy again. Now you'd have a much stronger feeling. Ahh, you'd say, this feels good; this feels safe. It's a wonderful, cozy, comfortable feeling.

But it has to be a feeling based on a fact. There has to be a real basis for that feeling. It can't be a pure leap in the dark. In this sense, trust is always a statement like, "I trust this because . . ." I trust my new doctor because she comes highly recommended. I trust this restaurant because it's been in business for a while and seems to have a lot of happy customers. I trust this person I'm dating because so far he seems honest and solid.

It's interesting. While trust is a feeling based on a fact, it's not a feeling based on certainty. We can't say that this new doctor will never and can never make a mistake. We can't say that nothing will ever go wrong in the kitchen of this restaurant. And we certainly can't say that this honest-and-solid-seeming person will never do anything to hurt us.

And that's the funny thing about trust. It has to be based on fact, but it can't be based on certainty, because we can never find that certainty. I know this can feel awfully hard to sort out, especially in relationships but the concept is pretty clear. When you say you trust someone, you have to have something that you can point to that makes your trust look reasonable, and there shouldn't be anything people could point to that would make your trust seem unreasonable. If you get involved with a guy who comes from a good family and has a responsible job, those are facts that point to him being trustworthy. At least it's a beginning. They don't make it certain you can trust him, but they certainly don't make your trust seem unreasonable, as would be the case if it were also a fact that he'd mistreated the women he'd previously been involved with.

All you can do is look for facts that make trust reasonable, and probe for facts that would make trust *un*reasonable. Then you know you're not taking a total leap into the dark. But there are still no guarantees.

A betrayal adds a new fact into the mixture. When someone betrays or disappoints you, you will more or less quickly come to believe that that person is flawed in such a way as to keep producing those disappointments. The bigger and more unusual the disappointment, the quicker you will come to that judgment.

So mistrust is a feeling based on a fact, too: anxiety because of a belief in unreliability. And that's where conflict in relationships comes in. Let's say I did something that hurt you. You trusted me, and now you don't. You thought I was reliable and now you think I'm unreliable. *But I don't think I'm unreliable.* I know I screwed up. But I don't think I *am* a screw-up.

And that's what we fight about. You're angry with me for being unreliable. And once I apologize and show you how sorry I am, if you're still angry with me, I'm going to start being angry with you for being so anxious.

THE ESSENCE OF THE BETRAYAL FIGHT. This is the basic fight between the person who's been betrayed and the person who has done the betraying. You feel you'll win if you can convince me of how unreliable I am. I feel I'll win if I can convince you of what an anxious ninny you are. I'll be trying to tell you to stop making such a big deal of the whole thing. And you'll be trying to tell me that the whole thing really is a big deal. We'll get polarized and things will escalate. You'll soon be talking to me as if you thought I was completely evil. And I'll be talking to you as if I thought you were completely insane.

It's really a fight over what the facts really are. Is it a fact that I'm unreliable? Or is it a fact that you're making a big deal over nothing? The way we live, who we are to each other, whether we have a future together—all this depends on which of these facts is real.

We'll become so angry and so far apart that any possibility of restoring trust will be blown out of the water, along with our relationship.

This dynamic is what we're up against when there's been a betrayal.

How to Heal a Relationship After a Major Betrayal

Suppose some poor schmo was sleeping peacefully in bed and someone came in, snatched him up, put a hood over his head, and took him to some unknown foreign city, where he was just left on the street. What a disorienting nightmare. He'd been sleeping safely in bed and knew exactly where he was, and now he is in a completely strange place.

I don't know about you, but if that was me, a whole bunch of questions would come to mind. Am I going to be okay? Where am I? How am I going to eat? Where am I going to sleep? How can I let people know where I am? How can I get back home?

These are key questions. But they are what stand between me being in a total nightmare and me feeling safe. If I can come up with good answers to these questions, everything will be okay.

THE SIX QUESTIONS. It works in a very similar way with a major betrayal. Here, too, we're completely disoriented. Here, too, we have to figure things out if we want to feel okay again. And, it turns out, here, too, there are six key questions.

If you've been betrayed in a big way by someone who's important to you, then knowing what these questions are and how to get answers to them will make all the difference in whether or not trust can be restored and the relationship can be rebuilt.

1. How will I ever cope with this?

2. Does the other person really care about me?

3. Can the other person really see me and understand how his betrayal hurt me?

4. Can our relationship survive?

5. Can we make things safer and better between us?

6. Can I forgive him?

It's much more likely that at the beginning, when you're so upset at discovering that you've been betrayed and feel you're going out of your mind, you'll be wondering if you can even cope with this. Forgiveness won't even seem like a remote possibility. But later on, after you've worked through a lot of issues, the possibility of forgiveness will loom as a very important question.

But please know that there is no timetable for this process. People vary and their circumstances vary.

The key point is this: It's only by getting answers to these questions that you can restore trust. The questions will show you the way. And I'll show you how to come up with good answers.

So now let's get started with the first question: *How will I ever cope with this?* As you know, if you're going through this yourself, what I'm really talking about is feeling like you're going out of your mind.

How Will I Ever Cope with This?

On June 23, 1993, a woman's husband came home drunk from a night of partying with the boys and forced her to have sex with him. I'm sure he didn't think it was rape, but she did, and so does the law now, thank goodness. And if nothing exactly like that has happened to you—and I hope it hasn't—I think most of us can relate to feeling forced to do something we didn't want to do, and where the pressure was so great, and the loss so great as well, that we felt betrayed.

Well, that woman certainly felt betrayed. This wasn't the first time her husband had taken her against her will. Something snapped in her. When her husband fell asleep in a drunken stupor, she got up, went to the kitchen, grabbed a knife, and cut off his penis. Still holding on to the severed penis, she went to her car and drove around for a while. Eventually she rolled the car window down and threw the penis into a vacant lot.

Somehow that brought her to her senses. She called 911 and entered the history books.

This was, of course, Lorena Bobbitt. She was arrested, held in jail, put on trial, and eventually found not guilty by reason of insanity. John Wayne Bobbitt got his penis back, but, needless to say, their marriage was over. (John Wayne Bobbitt was charged with abuse a number of times in later relationships, severely challenging the idea that people learn from experience.)

When they first heard what Lorena did, a lot of people cheered her on. This was the ultimate story of the victim finally getting back a little of her own. Police braced themselves for a wave of copycat crimes but they never materialized.

THE INCONCEIVABLE. When she whacked off his willy, Lorena was dealing with what most people go through when they are first hit by a major betrayal: *insanity*. At this stage it's normal to feel and act crazy. Why not? In a way, there is nothing worse than betrayal. If you're walking down a dark street and somebody robs you at gunpoint, well, that's awful, but it's not really a betrayal. In fact, it confirms our sense of the way things are in the world: There are bad people and you have to watch out for them. But suppose a friend somehow embezzles money from you. That's horrible, precisely because something like that is not supposed to happen. Bad guys rob you. Friends don't.

With betrayal, the inconceivable happened. Someone we trusted who was supposed to take care of us or be there for us, has hurt or abandoned us. *The world no longer makes any sense.* Something happened that's just crazy. And it makes sense that it would make you feel crazy. That's what betrayal feels like.

WHAT'S NORMAL. You may feel crazy, and I certainly did. You may act crazy, though I hope you don't. *But you're not actu-*

ally crazy. What you're feeling, what you're going through, is normal. You are normal. It's just that your life has gone crazy and you're responding to that craziness the way anybody would.

There's something about the power of betrayal that makes you feel that you can't trust anything anymore. This is why most people who've gone through a major betrayal talk about how they've never felt less safe or more helpless in their lives. It will pass, but feeling crazy can last many, many days or even weeks.

There's something to be said for going through the crazy stage. It is part of the natural healing process. I've seen people who won't let themselves go through it. They think they should be above these kinds of feelings. But it's almost as if there's a measure of craziness that just has to come out, and if it doesn't come out now it will leak out later when you're needing to be farther along in the trust-restoring process. Now is when everyone is expecting the crazy, so you might as well give it to them.

BEFORE IT'S TOO LATE. During this period you might find yourself doing things that you never in a million years thought you'd do. Or maybe you don't do anything. There are many forms of insanity, and they include shock and immobility. Some people just don't want to talk to anyone about anything during this phase.

Although some people do act crazy, the defining characteristic is confusion, wild thoughts alternating with no thoughts at all, an overpowering sense that you've entered an alternative, head-spinning reality.

FEELING CRAZY, OKAY; ACTING CRAZY, NOT OKAY

It makes sense that, when your world has suddenly been turned upside down and you're feeling you're going out of your mind, the big question is: How will I ever cope?

Of course right now you're feeling like you can't cope. So this is an important question that needs an answer.

WHAT'S AT STAKE: If you don't get a satisfying answer to this question, there's a serious risk that you'll never stop being stressed out and made frantic by this betrayal. I've seen this happen. People convince themselves that they can't cope, and then every time they are hit by a feeling of mistrust they completely lose it. But when you realize that you can cope, even if you're still upset, you can act in a constructive way.

So how will you ever cope? The answer is clear and I can give it to you now. **You _are_ coping.** This is what coping feels like right after a major betrayal. You're overwhelmed, and it shows. For the next brief period, coping is going to involve feeling disoriented, feeling that the world has spun out of control.

I can promise you this: If you just hang in there through this period, you will start having a clearer and stronger feeling that you actually are coping.

But there is real danger. Sometimes people don't cope. It's not because they're so upset. It's not even because they go through a period where they find it hard to function. Of course you're going to find it hard to function. But there is a major mistake people can make.

The mistake Lorena Bobbitt made, and the mistake you should never make, is to do something you can't take back.

Let's say you catch your husband cheating and throw him out of the house so he has to sleep in a motel for a few nights. That's a big deal, but it's not irrevocable. It's not something that does permanent harm. Compare that to Lorena Bobbitt or to a woman who caught her husband cheating and immediately called his boss and told him in detail all the ways her husband had been cheating his company. This not only cost her husband his job but his career. It hurt not only her husband but herself and her kids as well.

But, you might ask, if someone's betrayed you why not get back at him any way you can? Assuming you stay on the right side of the law, why not inflict back on him as much hurt as he caused you?

Well, we certainly feel like doing that. And those feelings are totally normal. But there's an excellent reason not to do it.

It might surprise you—and if you're going through this right now, you probably won't believe it—but the turmoil you're feeling has nothing to do with whether or not your relationship can heal or should heal. *It is just not true that the more pain you feel, the more that means your relationship is better off dead.* It could even mean the opposite. I've seen many situations where the initial pain from betrayal was mostly caused by the feeling that, "How could you have done what you did when we had so many good things going for us?"

So the reason not to do anything you might regret is that once the dust has settled there is a very good chance that you will want to continue in this relationship. Not as it was, of course. Not without making sure that whatever caused the betrayal is dealt with. Not without working hard to rebuild trust. But still the relationship may be well worth saving.

It's not the size of the betrayal that kills a relationship. It's the weakness of the relationship itself that makes it vulnerable when a betrayal occurs. And that's why it's all the more important not to do anything you'll regret during this initial crazy stage. That's the only mistake you have to worry about at this point. Things will be crazy and messy and awful, but people and relationships can and do recover from that all the time. Just don't do anything you'll regret.

YOUR WISEST FRIEND. To help you cope, and to help you make sure that you don't do anything you'll regret, do this. It's the single most important thing you can do to cope while you're feeling you're out of your mind. Figure out who your wisest, sanest, most level-headed friend is and talk to her. She may not be your best friend. Let's face it, many of us have best friends who are pretty crazy. This can be a lot of fun when you're not going through a crisis. But now you are going through a crisis and that's a whole new ballgame.

So talk to your sanest friend, and whatever you're thinking of doing, run it by her first. "I'm thinking of setting his car on fire. What do you think?" Hopefully your sanest friend will recognize that this is a bad idea and talk you out of it.

Sometimes coping means knowing where you're having trouble and then finding someone to help you cope with it.

* * *

IF YOU STILL have any kind of relationship left by the time you start being a little less crazy, you're in good shape. If there was no glue holding you together, the craziness of this phase would blow you apart. If you're not blown apart, it means there is some glue, some degree of caring, and that makes all the difference here. Believe it or not, the trust-restoring has begun.

You've answered your first question. You've shown you can cope.

7

Discovering That the Other Person Actually Cares

THERE'S SOMETHING THAT betrayers usually don't understand. They think—because they so want it to be true—that after the initial discovery and flare up, there's a steady cooling down. Ah, if only it were that simple. But the fact is that as the craziness dies down, what people are aware of feeling, more than anything else, is anger, and that anger may actually grow hotter and wilder. It comes as a shock to discover that the end of craziness doesn't mean the end of anger. It's often the prelude.

Instead of things getting better, for a while things seem to get worse. But it would be a mistake to think that anger is always hot. The anger some people fall into can have a cold feel to it. It's not always like a bunch of firecrackers that go off but eventually are exhausted; it's sometimes more like an ice age. There's a huge glacier of anger and it doesn't seem to melt at all.

Either way, hot or cold, anger is the part of the aftermath of betrayal that people most expect yet find hardest to deal with. But as you'll see, anger can be an important part of the trust-restoring process.

Lily and Boris

Lily and Boris had been saving money for quite a while. It was supposed to be for a down payment for a house. At least that's what Lily thought, and so for her this was sacred, untouchable money. Evidently, though, Boris, her husband, hadn't gotten the memo, or perhaps he just didn't take it so seriously. One day she checked into their account and to her horror she discovered that half of it had disappeared. He told her he'd spent it on instruments for the guys in his band and for some recording sessions. It added up to a lot of money.

The insanity stage hit Lily as a kind of sickness. She went to bed as if taken with the plague. She kept thinking, "We'll never have a home now." But it wasn't just that the money was gone. This was supposed to be something they were working for together. They were supposed to be partners but it now seemed clear to her that they weren't close or connected or even a couple anymore.

But the confusion eventually drifted away and gave way to intense anger. How *dare* he, Lily thought. Lily felt the kind of rage she thought only came over women who were protecting their children from attack. And in a way that made sense here—there was something vulnerable and innocent and precious in their hopes and plans and in the trust she'd felt that what mattered to her mattered to him as well. And now all that was violated.

DO YOU REALLY CARE ABOUT ME?

We're so used to the idea that someone gets angry after they've been betrayed, that we don't ask why. Isn't it obvious?

Not at all. For example—and I know this is going to sound crazy to you—but once the initial upset dies down, the dominant feeling could be gratitude. Think about it for a moment: Maybe the relationship wasn't all that great before the betrayal. Maybe you had the occasional thought of leaving. Then the other person does whatever it is he does and you think, Good, now I've got your true colors. I know who you really are. Thank you. You've saved me a lot of time.

And you know what? I have seen people respond exactly like this. But of course it is an unusual response. So why is anger the dominant response?

Because anger is not just a feeling. It's a tactic. Nature is too thrifty to give us creatures feelings that aren't useful. We have the feelings that we do because they accomplish something.

And in the context of betrayal, anger accomplishes something huge. It enables us to answer the next big question that haunts us as we're trying to deal with the betrayal: *Do you really care about me?*

This is a tremendously important question. It deals with the essence of the betrayal and it gets at the heart of whether healing the mistrust is possible or not.

WHAT'S AT STAKE: If you can't get to the point where you feel that the other person really cares about you, then you probably won't be able to get back into this relationship. Why would you be in a relationship with someone you know doesn't care about you? If you do stay, you'll never feel loved. But when you do realize that the other person cares about you, however ignorant, confused, and clumsy he may be, then you'll have the motivation you need to rebuild trust.

Almost everyone feels that betrayal is a sign that the other person doesn't care. If the other person really cared about you, he couldn't possibly have done what he did, could he?

But there's a whole other aspect to this, which I know about from working with countless couples where one has betrayed the other. Yes, if this person had cared more, she wouldn't have betrayed you. But strangely enough this doesn't necessarily mean she doesn't care. Sometimes people care about you but they're angry. Sometimes people care about you but they get confused or distracted. Sometimes people care about you but they go stupid.

So it's a *fact* that someone can do something that makes it look as though she doesn't care—and for sure she wasn't caring when she did that thing—but nonetheless, fundamentally, she really does care.

In fact, that was the very first thing Boris talked about when Lily found out what he'd done. He talked about how sorry he was, how he'd never meant to hurt her, how important she was to him, how he would do everything in the world to make it up to her. "Look, I'm just a dickhead," he said, "but you're everything to me and I'll fix this. I promise."

Of course at that point Lily told Boris she didn't believe him, and she meant it. "You're just a selfish bastard," she said, "and the only person you care about is yourself."

That's what Lily said, and she said it because she was letting her anger accomplish one of the things nature gave us anger to accomplish: scare the crap out of Boris so that he would think twice about hurting her again.

But she was also doing something else, of far greater long-run importance. She was trying to figure out who was right. Was Boris right when he said he cared? Or was she right in feeling that he didn't care?

Now let me ask you: How would you go about figuring this out?

THE DO-YOU-CARE TEST

Of course caring is easy when it doesn't really require anything. Every animal shelter has cages full of puppies and kittens who were given up because someone cared; they just didn't care enough. They wanted a cute little pet, but real animals poop and puke and require time and attention. Not being able to give the animal what it needs is a sign that the person didn't really care. Not enough, anyway.

And it works the same way when there's been a betrayal. All hell breaks loose because the person who's been betrayed is just a quivering mass of safety needs. This is not a fun person to be with. This is most of us at our absolute worst—quite understandably, of course—and the yelling and storming around and making demands can go on for quite a while.

But if the person who betrayed you can hang in there while you're furious, he's passed the do-you-care test. Think about it. You've been incredibly difficult—for weeks! months! and yet he hasn't walked out. That's what we look for: this sign of his commitment to you, to the relationship, and to the healing process. If the betrayer can hang in there, you know that there's a foundation of caring that can give you solid trust. You've gotten the answer to your question: He really does care.

And if he doesn't hang in there, you've still gotten an answer to your question. He doesn't care. That's sad news, but it's not a surprise, and at least now you know. He really doesn't care, so you're really free to move on.

By using a long period of anger as a way of discovering whether the other person cares about us or not, we're really putting the other person through a kind of trial by ordeal. Anyone can understand this. You put me through hell so if you're not willing to go through hell yourself, you don't really care about me.

I'm not saying we do this in a deliberate, manipulative way. (Though some of us do!) Mostly this just happens. We're just angry. Our anger is not part of a plan, it's just a response to our pain. But it does have the effect of setting up a situation so that we get a really good answer *we can trust* to the question *Do you care about me?*

Anger Is More Than a Big, Loud Noise

There's an aspect to anger as a test for whether the other person really cares about you that can be confusing. Anger can come out in ways that mask its true nature. You can be expressing anger without your being aware that you're putting the other person to the test and without his being aware that he's being put to the test.

Rather than yelling and screaming, anger can come out in the form of coldness and distance. You might be feeling angry, but the other person might think you're calming down. And although your words are not loud and frantic, they can be brutally cruel.

Lily was so devastated by Boris's betrayal that she told him, "You've totally lost it as a musician. Nobody thinks you're any good anymore. Your friends just laugh at you behind your back. You're just a hack and I don't respect you." There was just enough truth in what she said that he believed her completely. He couldn't feel safe in her presence again. What's more, he found it impossible to trust his friends. This was tremendously destructive.

THE GRILLING/VENTING PROCESS. Another way anger comes out is during what I call *the grilling/venting process*. This is one of the most common features of the anger test. In it, the betrayer is subjected to what seems like an infinite number of questions, and every answer he gives is wrong and leads to a tirade and to more questions. Being subjected to the grilling/venting process feels like torture.

Just between you and me, I subjected my husband to the grilling/venting process for at least a couple of months. I can't honestly say I was completely unaware of the torture aspect of this. We want to torture our betrayer a bit. After all, his telling me about his emotional affair tortured me; of course I wanted to torture him back. I'm not proud of it, but this is how we work, and if we want to have healing after a betrayal we have to understand what's really going on.

But another aspect of this process is quite genuine. We really do have a million questions, and the answers we get really do seem lame. We need a lot more than we're getting, and so of course we ask these questions over and over again.

I've often asked myself why we do this. Let's face it, most of the time we either know the answer, or we know that the answer doesn't really matter, or we know that the other person doesn't know the answer himself.

For example, Lily must have asked Boris 832 times *WHY* he spent their money the way he did without asking her. And what happened to them is interesting because it's what happens to most of us when we go through the grilling/venting process.

First, Boris said he didn't know. Lily blew up. That answer seemed so idiotic and evasive. She told him of course he knew. Boris really didn't think he knew, but she was so enraged he just wanted to placate her. So he said the first thing he could think of: "I didn't think you'd mind." This answer seemed even more idiotic. It just couldn't be true. It made her frantic that she was married to such an idiot. So she blew up even more. The more upset she got, the more desperate Boris became and the more he tried to come up with the answer he thought she was looking for. His answers started having even less of a ring of truth; plus, they started sounding just plain weird.

At one point, thinking that this was the kind of psychological answer that would make her happy, Boris said, "Well, maybe I did it to get back at you."

"For what!?!" Lily shouted.

"Shit," Boris thought. *"I hadn't gotten this far in my thinking. I have no idea why I might want to get back at her. I better make something up."* So once again Boris said the first thing that came into his head: "Maybe I did it to get back at you for putting on weight."

This was not a good direction to go in. Boris's "honesty," even though it was made up on the spot, did not impress her. She just felt even more humiliated, even more wronged. She blew up again. A transcript of Boris saying something stupid in his desperation and Lily blowing up, giving him a tongue lashing, and then pressuring him to say something even more idiotic could easily take up this whole book. I'll spare you that.

WHY DO WE DO THIS? I think there are a lot of reasons why we do this. For one thing, remember: *We're angry!* Even if we knew that the grilling/venting process was a waste of time, it would still feel worth it just to be able to feel that we're inflicting pain back on the person who inflicted pain on us. That might not be attractive or noble, but it is the way people work.

For another thing, when we've been betrayed we have, after all, been through the most disorienting, foundation-shaking experience a person can have. Our whole world has turned to Jell-O. One of the first questions people who've been caught in a betrayal always get asked is, "What else are you hiding from me?" But we take this uncertainty further afield. We wonder what dark betrayals *other* people in our lives have in store for us.

Somehow, we think, with our last shred of hopefulness, if we get answers then that will make things okay. And that's not an altogether loopy notion. Most people, for example, feel better when they finally get a diagnosis for a mysterious condition, even when the diagnosis isn't a particularly favorable one. Somehow, we just feel better when we know.

Of course when we question someone who's betrayed us we don't get the certainty we're looking for. We get what seem like lies or evasions. But instead of abandoning the search for answers we press on even harder. We're so convinced that we'll explode if we don't get the truth that we press on no matter what.

When something bad is happening to us there's something about the human psyche that makes us need to know *why*. I'll never forget hearing a 911 tape of a woman being attacked by a man with a knife. It went on for many minutes. He kept stabbing her and she kept trying to get away. And the whole time this nightmare was going on, she kept screaming, *"Why? Why? Why?"* over and over hundreds of times until he'd killed her.

We need to *understand*, even with our very last breath. It's just the way people work.

And you know what? There are answers to our questions. With time and patience and good collaboration, the two of you can tease out an understanding of what went on that led to the betrayal. But this understanding never comes during the anger stage. The anger poisons the atmosphere so it's not safe to either speak or hear the truth. But the good news is that if both people can hang in there and if the anger doesn't blow the relationship apart, you can communicate well enough to uncover the truth.

COMPLAINING. Very, very often anger comes out in the form of complaining. This too makes sense. After all, when someone's been betrayed, they've been victimized. And being victimized means being treated like a nothing. If someone points a gun at you and steals your wallet, they're giving you the message that your life, your feelings, your property, your future happiness mean nothing to them. You're just a thing. And it's a terrible shock for any of us to be treated like a thing. We may be paralyzed in the moment, but we will go forward needing to be treated like a whole person.

That's why we complain. It's our way of saying, "If you'd thought about me, you wouldn't have done what you did. But you did it. So clearly you weren't thinking about me. I was just a big nothing to you. Well, no more. Now I'm going to show you how much of a person I am." And out the words come, on and on, seemingly endlessly.

But if the other person can hang in there and listen, then maybe, we think, he cares about me.

ENTERING THE DANGER ZONE

So this is what we do. Once the craziness dies down, the anger settles in, and we usually stay angry for a long time. From the point of view of trying to feel safe, this is a very smart tactic. Angry people are scary people. You don't want to mess with an angry person. You want to hunker down and stay out of their way.

In fact, when you're with someone who's really angry you want to get as far away as possible. You might want to get so far away that you have nothing more to do with that person.

And so anger destroys relationships. And it doesn't allow for trust to rebuild either. Now you might say, what do I care if the person who betrayed me trusts me? I want him to be scared of me so he'll never hurt me again.

I understand. When I was betrayed I was sure I was the angriest woman who'd ever lived, and part of me thought that wasn't a totally bad thing. But just the way you can't trust an angry person, you can't trust someone who is trying to cope with an angry person. The fact is that if someone is really angry, or always likely to become angry, we're more likely to lie to that person or to hide things from him. Why not? We don't want to deal with his anger!

So we have to face the possibility, the fact actually, that from the point of view of rebuilding trust, anger is a big mistake. Yes, it makes you feel safer to get angry, but it also makes for distance and deviousness and resentment and it undermines loyalty, and these are the last things you want if you want to get to the place where you can really trust each other again.

Sure, anger is normal and understandable. To some degree it's unavoidable. But I beg you to listen to what I'm about to say: I caused an incredible amount of damage in my relationship with my anger, both because of how angry I got and because of how long I stayed angry. And I've since validated this with all the couples and families I've worked with. **The less anger we indulge in, the faster healing happens.**

Some anger is normal and inevitable. Beyond that, the less anger there is, the better. Too much anger creates a dysfunctional ordeal. Anger is a test that can be pushed too far.

ANGER PUSHED TOO FAR

If you're the person who's been betrayed and wants to find a way to trust again, there is danger for you here. It's true that your anger is a test of the other person's caring. But it's also a test of the other person's ability to withstand discouragement. And let's face facts, you and me, since we've both gone through a betrayal. Our anger—the intensity of it, the way it can seem to go on and on—can be very discouraging to the other person.

We've all said things like, "I don't know how I'll ever be able to trust you again." We say that in part as a plea for hope: Please give me something that will make it possible for me to trust you again. But our partner is likely to hear it very differently, as a kind of long-term weather forecast: In my opinion, I don't think I'll ever be able to trust you again.

So the danger to you is that your partner will get to a point like this (and these words are taken, with a few changes to help protect his privacy, from an email a guy sent to his wife):

I love you, and I will always love you. I'm so sorry for what I did. If chopping off my arm could turn back the clock and make it so that what I did never happened, I would do so. In spite of this, I don't see how I can keep going on with you. You keep making it abundantly clear that you will never be able to get past this. I know you've been incredibly hurt and angry, but I thought that would have started to die down by now. It hasn't. I don't know what you want from me. I do know you've told me over and over that you will never be able to trust me again. So I guess at this point I'm going to have to take you at your word. I would give anything for us not to be in this place, but I just don't see any point in my hanging in there any longer. You've told me there's no point.

But here's what this guy didn't know. His wife was still in an emotional state. She was still focused on her anger. She was still hungry to know that he cared.

And so she made a terrible mistake. She thought that her hurt and his crime made it safe for her to indulge in anger for as long as she wanted and in any way she wanted. But she was wrong and when she found out her mistake, it was too late.

You have a total right to find out whether the other person cares. But you're not finding out what you need if you push the test past anyone's point of endurance.

How Much Is Too Much?

Where do you draw the line and say that's too much anger? That's a tough question. I am so leery of telling somebody who's been terribly hurt that she's gone over the limit.

I sure wouldn't have appreciated anyone telling that to me when I was caught up in being angry with my husband. But I'm torn.

I know we don't want to be told to contain our anger, especially when it feels so justified. And I know that it doesn't work to simply tell someone, "Don't be angry."

But I also know, as a matter of well-established fact, that too much anger is toxic. It damages the relationship and prevents trust from being restored.

So without my telling you what to do, let me share with you a timetable that I train therapists to use. It's a timetable that will let you see when your anger may have gone past the normal limits. Now, I understand: "normal" is a very controversial word. But I'm just using it here in the statistical sense. I'm just saying that if you go off this timetable, then you're expressing much more anger than most people do who are dealing with the same awful betrayal that you're dealing with. And so if your anger is off the charts, then you've got to be willing to at least look at the possibility of doing things to dial it back, and I'll show you just how to do that.

So here is the post-betrayal timetable for normal anger:

By the end of the first month
There's still pretty much unlimited anger here. *But* there should also be two other things. Just occasionally, there should be a tiny bit of cooling off. Your anger shouldn't be white-hot the entire month. And your anger shouldn't be so intense that you're doing crazy things to hurt yourself or the other person.

By the end of the first three months
You should be at the point where you can have a sane, productive conversation with the other person for the purpose of accomplishing some joint goal. You should be able, for example,

to do something like make a meal together, take the kids to the park, have friends over, or pay bills together without a fight and without it feeling like a tense ordeal. You may still be feeling that you're under a cloud of anger, but it doesn't affect or infect everything.

By the end of the first six months

You may still be aware that anger is an issue in your relationship. You may very well still have flashes of anger. Sometimes they will come out of nowhere. There may be a lingering feeling of walking on eggshells. But anger should no longer be your usual operating mode. It should feel as though you're not angry more often than you are angry.

By the end of the first year

There may still be occasional flashes of anger, especially when something re-stimulates your feelings around the betrayal. But generally speaking, you'd have to say that you're no longer angry. As far as the relationship is concerned, although you still don't completely feel that trust has been restored, you do feel that you're on the way.

By the end of the first two years

Anger is mostly gone, trust has been restored (at least you can act as if you trust each other), and your relationship is as good as if not better than it was before the betrayal. You can now talk about the betrayal without getting angry and upset.

I have to say that in my experience, the timetable I've outlined has more anger going on for longer than is healthy. You need to know that. But it's still okay. It's within the normal range. But if you go beyond this timetable, then the anger is really unhealthy.

It's your choice. If you don't want healing to happen, then let it all hang out. Forget what's healthy. Forget the timetable. Believe me, the healing won't happen. And maybe that's how you want to end the relationship. Lots of people do. They don't want it to be: You betray me, we're over. They want it to be: You betray me, I put you through hell, then we're over.

But if this is a test to see if the other person really cares, you have to ask yourself: If you put the betrayal aside, has this been a good relationship, or at least a good enough relationship? If it has been, why wouldn't you want to try to see if you can heal it? If it hasn't been a good relationship, why bother? Remember, the hell you put the other person through is hell for you, too.

Grace and Wendy

When Grace had been diagnosed with breast cancer, her oldest and best friend, Wendy, abandoned her. She simply refused to answer any of Grace's calls or texts. This might seem inconceivable to you, and it was inconceivable to Grace as well. That's part of what made it so shocking. When Grace ran into her at the supermarket and confronted her, Wendy said she had a terrible phobia about cancer. Even hearing someone talk about it made her afraid she was going to get it. Wendy turned her back on Grace and walked away.

Grace eventually made a full recovery from cancer. Wendy heard of this and tried to reach out to her. But by this point Grace was too angry to do anything but refuse to talk to her.

Grace asked me a question I've heard from countless people.

"You say my anger is starting to damage my relationship. But how the hell do I turn down the anger? It's just how I feel." In fact, it made Grace angry with me that I would even hint at the possibility that she should feel less angry. People feel so strongly that their anger is self-protective that they often get furious at the thought of it being taken away.

It's a real puzzle, isn't it. We recognize that anger is normal. We feel entitled to our anger. In some way, we feel comforted by our anger. And yet we also realize that our anger is hurting us.

So what do we do? We can't just turn off our feelings.

But I'm *not* asking you to stop being angry. If you want to burn that no-good, cheating, rat-bastard to a crisp with the searing heat of your anger, go for it. Anger is both natural and inevitable. But you have to be aware of how your anger can blow up in your face.

WATCH OUT FOR THE ANGER CYCLE. The other person, let's say it's your spouse, gets it that you're going to be angry. He knows he's really hurt you and pissed you off. He's expecting a period where there's going to be a lot of anger. That's your window. But it's a smaller window than you might think or than you would like. After all, no one likes to deal with rage, so while he recognizes your need for anger, he's not so keen on letting it boil for an extended period of time.

So your spouse will go along for a while, and not only up to the point where he can't take it anymore, but for even longer than that, because of his guilt. In other words, he's going to be fed up with hearing your anger before he lets you know it. You are, in short, creating a walking time bomb. Eventually, and sooner than you might think, he will blow up at you. Not because he's justified in doing so, but because he's a normal human being.

In its mildest form this could come out with your spouse saying, angrily, "When are you going to get over this?" It's as if he's saying, Okay, you've gone way past the point of being legitimately injured and now you're just milking this. And of course you're going to respond to this by getting . . . even more furious!

This is the **anger cycle**, and you need to be aware of it, because it is very dangerous. Anger breeds anger. And in my experience the anger cycle kicks in *before* most people reach the point that the timetable indicates is normal anger.

In a perfect world, what anger should be is information. Anger is a gift nature gave animals and us so we could signal to each other, "See? This is a really big deal for me." It's as if there's this anger-o-meter which lets us show people how much things matter to us. That's when we express anger.

But when we're on the receiving end of it, we experience anger as control and abuse. No one likes to be yelled at, even when they realize that the anger is justified. So when your partner gets angry back at you, he's not responding to your legitimate need to let him know what a big deal it was that you were hurt. He's responding to feeling controlled and abused.

And you're going to respond exactly the same way. Even if you accept that it's been tough for him living with an angry person, you're going to feel controlled and abused by his anger and you're going to get even angrier back at him.

HOW IT ENDS. Here's the dangerous thing about the anger cycle: It doesn't contain a mechanism in itself for dying down. It either escalates or keeps going at a pretty high level.

There are only two ways the anger cycle ends. One way is when it kills the relationship. In this sense it's like a cancer. When a cancer kills someone, the cancer dies, too, but it doesn't care because it's a purely destructive force. And it's the same with the anger cycle.

The other way the anger cycle ends is when it brings you to such a crazy place that you have to stop and say, Whoa, this is just crazy. What are we doing to each other?

The problem is that once you've hopped on the crazy train it's hard to turn around, even when you realize where you are. Sure, you may recognize that your anger has led you into a very bad place. But it's really hard to forget the things that the other person has said and done in his anger.

I'm telling you all this because it makes me sad to think of all the couples who've come to me with their relationships already destroyed by the anger cycle. They got on the crazy train and couldn't get off. This *never* makes sense. If they'd wanted the relationship to end, they could have done so without this enormous waste of time and without all this pain. But most of these people were wanting to keep their relationship alive. Sadly, in some cases it was too late. The anger cycle had done them in.

So I am asking you to be aware.

Be aware that this anger you're feeling is just a stage. It's not the truth. It's just an uncomfortable place you happen to be in now, like a long flight. It will pass. And when it does, I promise you, you will regret all the time you spent and all the misery you went through in this angry place.

And be aware of what this anger is all about. By being betrayed, you were made to feel very small, almost like a nothing. And now you want to make yourself seem big, someone to be reckoned with. And of course you're doing this to feel safe. The scarier you are, the less likely you think anyone is to mess with you.

And that leads to the next thing you need to be aware of. *What do you want?* I understand: You probably don't know. It's hard to know. For one thing, you're too angry to think clearly! But as long as there might just be the possibility that you will want to rebuild this relationship and restore trust, then that has to be at least part of what you want.

And so if there's even just a possibility that you might want to stay in this relationship, be aware of how destructive your anger can be.

GETTING OFF THE ANGER TRAIN

Now you might be saying, Okay, okay, okay, I get it: too much anger is bad. But how do I stop? I'm still really angry!

Good question. There are a lot of things you can do that work to prevent the anger you need to see if the other person really cares from going too far and poisoning your relationship. I suggest you do as many of them as you can.

- You can keep an anger journal and vent to your heart's content there.

- You can vent about the betrayal to a friend or a counselor or a therapist or a clergy person. That way you're getting your anger out but you're not causing harm. It's much, much easier to hear someone's anger if it's not directed at you.

- You can work out an agreement with your partner, letting
  him know you still need to express your anger but giving him permission to not deal with it. One of my clients
  told her husband, "Look, I still need to vent, so how about
  if I send you angry emails when my anger has built up. I'll
  put 'venting' in the subject line. I'd like you to read them,
  but you don't have to. I'm not going to quiz you on them."
  It was a great tool for them. It allowed her to release her
  anger and gave her partner the opportunity to just hit de-
  lete when he needed a break from it.

Be honest with yourself: Is this anger really all about the
betrayal? Many of us carry around a ton of anger. Some of it goes
back to ways we were deprived or mistreated when we were kids.
Some of it comes from our work and career. Everyone I know
has been bullied and abused in some way by someone or something, and that makes us angry. But we don't have an outlet for
expressing it. Then someone betrays us and all this rage comes
out. Some from the betrayal and some—maybe a lot—from
anger at previous hurts and grievances.

If this is true for you, why not go into therapy to help you
deal with it?

I am not saying that you need to be in therapy *just* because
someone betrayed you and made you angry. That anger is normal and healthy. Sometimes the person who's hurt you will suggest you go into therapy just so he won't have to deal with your
anger. To which I say, Tough. You created this monster, mister,
so now deal with it.

But if you would have to admit that your anger is unhealthy
or unproductive, then maybe therapy would help you. That way

you can find out if your partner really cares without destroying the relationship in the process.

Maybe, just maybe you can attach a filter to your mouth. Say what you want in anger, but hold back on the words that you know will hurt. This isn't easy, and I can't tell you where to draw the line. But I do know this: Most of us know the difference between words said in anger and words meant to hurt.

For example, say, "I hate you for what you did." This is just another way of saying that you're really, really angry, which the other person already knows. But don't say, "You know the real reason I married you? It was because I felt sorry for you."

Or, for example, say, "You were such a jerk." Everybody knows they've been a jerk from time to time. But don't say, "Before she died, your mother told me she never really loved you."

You get the point.

When we've been betrayed, we've been hurt in such a deep and personal way that of course we want to hurt back. But if you go down that road, you may destroy the very relationship that you might want again once your pain dies down.

You can also use something called "having a Vesuvius." (Mount Vesuvius was the volcano that exploded two thousand years ago and destroyed the Roman city of Pompeii. That was one angry volcano!) To do this, say to your partner, "I need to get some of my anger off my chest. How long can you listen?" The other person will say, "Two minutes," or something like that. Then you hand the person your watch and say, "Tell me when to go and tell me when my time is up." Then you can just let loose.

You have a time frame in which to let out as much anger as you want. But the other person doesn't feel assaulted because he's agreed to do this and because he's in control of the time. Also, you need to have the rule that anything you say during your Vesuvius is just your feelings. It's not necessarily reality. You can even say, "I wish you were dead." But in the framework of a Vesuvius, it's just an expression of your feelings; you do not actually mean that you wish the other person were dead. A Vesuvius is great because you can have all the anger you want and yet it doesn't put you on the crazy train.

You can just leave the room when you find the anger is building up. Just say you have to go to the bathroom. When you're there, splash cold water on your face. Then ask yourself that key question, What do I want? If you decide after you've thought about it calmly for a few minutes that you still want to go in there and dump all over your partner, well, then, at least it's a decision you've made and not just something that's swept you away.

I've found that when you give yourself a time-out, the need to express your anger dies down. And I'll tell you something that I wish I'd understood better when I was going through all this. Unexpressed anger doesn't give you ulcers or tumors. It doesn't fester and turn rancid. There's no evidence for that whatsoever. It's not like a chicken bone that sticks in your craw until you spit it out. It's not a poison that you have to get out of your system. It's none of these things.

Anger is just a feeling. It's like when you're watching TV and you see an ad for pizza and you suddenly have to have some. In the moment, the urgency is almost overwhelming. (Believe me, I know this all too well.) But if you don't do anything about that feeling, nothing will happen. It will just go away. And it works the same way with anger.

You can give the other person some idea of what you want in the midst of all your anger. We all have unmet needs in our relationships that come out in the aftermath of a betrayal. Somehow your fury with your husband over his accidentally throwing away your wedding pictures will get connected to your anger with him over only doing the fun parts of the kids' bedtime. He gets to read the stories while you clean up their mess. Well, that's an unmet need and it's sure to come out during one of your tirades. And that's good because it's a need that can get met if you discuss it and will make both of you feel less helpless.

That's important because life after a betrayal makes everyone feel helpless and discouraged. It's like you've entered this painful fog and nothing you do makes it go away. No wonder relationships die in this period. Human beings try to get away from whatever makes them feel discouraged.

But if you can say what you need, then you can help create an atmosphere of proactive problem-solving that's inspiring instead of discouraging.

Just one thing, though. If you're going to express a need, be specific. You can't just say, "Be nice to me," even if that's how you feel. Just saying those words isn't going to give anyone a clue about what to do. You've got to dig a little deeper. What would make you feel that the other person was being nice to you? If he smiled more often? If he helped around the house more? If he didn't interrupt you when you complained about what a rough day you've had at work? *Those* things are specific. And so you're more likely to get them and more likely to feel that the other person is giving you what you need.

If you do nothing else, you can at the very least let the other person know what your anger is really all about. It's not your anger in and of itself that makes your partner discouraged—it's his not understanding what's going on. You can be angry, but you need to put it in context. At some point when you're not quite so consumed with anger, you could say something like this: "Look, I know this is hard on you, too. And I wish I had some kind of timetable or road map that would tell me when my anger will start to die down. But I just don't know when that will happen. I do know that I want it to happen. I want to find a way to trust you again. And I know you want to be trustworthy. But here's the thing. When you hurt me, that gave me the message that you don't care about me. That I wasn't worth your caring about me. But if you can hang in there with me while I'm still so angry, that will tell me that you do care, and that means everything to me."

Saying something like this will allow you to have your anger, will allow you to see if the other person cares enough about you to stick around through it, but will prevent the terrible possibility that his discouragement will destroy your relationship.

And finally and most important, you can focus on getting what you need to feel safe.

Here's how this works. We've said that anger can be seen as a tool to help you figure out if the other person cares. But as you know, anger also springs from the part of us that doesn't feel safe.

There are lots of possible reasons for this, besides the betrayal itself. It could be the anger cycle. Suppose you need for the other person to be open for you to feel safe? Fine. But if you've been pretty angry for a long time, then even if you're within the time-table for what's normal, he may not feel safe opening up to you because he doesn't want to deal with your anger. You're unintentionally preventing yourself from getting the very thing you need.

It could also be—and I see this all the time—that the two of you just have not worked out an understanding so that he can give you what you need to feel safe. Maybe he doesn't know what you need. Maybe he knows what you need but he doesn't know how to do it. Maybe he knows how to do it but there's another reason why he's unable or unwilling to do it.

For example, he may not know how important it is to you for him to tell you about his relationships with the women he works with. Or he may know it but may then just inundate you with trivia. Or he may be reluctant to share with you the fact that he likes and is professionally close to some of his women colleagues—he may not understand that this is okay with you; you just want to know what's going on.

His knowing what you need to feel safe is something you need to collaborate on. It's in both of your interests. You want to feel safe, and he wants you to feel safe because then his life will be better, too.

There is still another possibility for why you still feel so unsafe: It's that the other person can't or won't do what you need to feel safe. Some people are just limited. Some people have the attitude of, Hey, this is who I am, this is how I roll, take it or leave it. Well, if there ever was a signal to leave, this is it. You can never rebuild trust with someone who can't or won't work with you to feel safe.

But think of the flip side. Suppose you manage to put out there what you need to feel safe and the other person does a fair job of meeting that need. Now you're way ahead of the game. Now you've not only healed the broken trust, but you've also healed your relationship.

This is such an important point that I want you to go back and reread the previous paragraph, because it has to do with why healing broken trust is so tricky and so important. You see, trust is not just one of many important ingredients in a healthy relationship. It's not just something nice that's not really vital. If this were your body, trust isn't like hair. Most of us want to have hair, but we don't really need it. No, trust is like your heart. Without your heart, you're not going to have a body. Your body can't function without a heart.

A RELATIONSHIP CAN'T FUNCTION WITHOUT TRUST. Just the way the heart nourishes every part of the body, trust nourishes the relationship. Let's say it's Sunday morning and you're lying around in bed reading the paper, sipping coffee, and casually talking. How can you do that without trust? If you don't trust each other, you'll be watching every moment for an attack or a painful and scary revelation. You'll be watching your own words and wary of the other person's. If something you hear strikes you the wrong way, you'll bristle and strike back.

And that's how feeling unsafe creates more lack of safety. This is *the mistrust cycle*. Mistrust creates prickliness. Prickliness causes harsh reactions. Harsh reactions cause more mistrust.

But if you put out there what you need to feel safe, *only good things will happen.* Either you'll get what you need to feel safe and so you'll break the mistrust cycle and feel the other person cares. Or you won't get it, and you'll know that the other person can't give you what you need to feel safe. Which means he either doesn't care or isn't able to do what will make you feel cared for.

Either way, you'll have gotten the answer to your question, Does he really care about me?

ZIPPING ALONG ON THE ROAD TO RESTORING TRUST

By now, I hope you're beginning to see and believe that broken trust can be restored.

For one thing, by focusing on your anger as a way for the other person to show he really cares about you, you can moderate your anger and avoid the time-wasting and destructive anger cycle. Some anger is inevitable. Some, we now know, is useful. But more than that is a destructive waste.

For another thing, dealing constructively with your anger prevents discouragement. Have you ever tried to walk through deep mud? It's very discouraging. You can barely make progress, and what progress you make is exhausting. The mud almost literally feels as if it's your enemy as it tries to suck you down. Well, that's what we get after trust has been broken. You're both deeply discouraged. You're discouraged because you're finding it hard to feel more trusting. The other person's discouraged because he can't do anything to shake you loose from your mistrust.

This discouragement is a serious risk factor. It's easy to start questioning if the relationship is even worth it. And when there's too much anger, and when it starts to take on a life of its own, sometimes people come to the conclusion, why bother? Rebuilding trust doesn't seem worth it. It doesn't even seem possible.

That's not the feeling you want to create in your partner. You want him to feel that rebuilding trust *is* possible, especially since he's the one who damaged your trust in the first place. And for that, he's got to see that your anger isn't infinite and uncontrollable.

Here's how one of my clients put it.

Cheating on Lindsey was the worst thing I've ever done, and I hate myself for having done it. Honestly, if I could chop off my arm and make it so that I'd never done it, I would do so. And right now with Lindsey not trusting me at all, I'm willing to do anything to win back her trust. She can monitor my computer. Track me using my cell phone. I get it. But the thing is . . . it's not that she's so angry. She has a right to be angry! It's just that . . . it's like her anger has taken on a life of its own. It's bottomless. And then I just can't help thinking, what's the point? If she'll never ever stop being angry, why am I doing all these things? I know I'm the one who made the mess, but if it can never be cleaned up, then why try?

But all this is avoided if you deal with anger the way I've suggested. By finding out whether the other person cares or not and by avoiding discouragement, you can make progress faster than you thought.

8

Feeling Seen

CASSIE AND LOU sat in front of me. He was crying and she was looking at him with a pained but cold expression. He'd gone on and on, sobbing about what a terrible thing he'd done when he'd cheated on her with their nanny, and yet somehow none of this had gotten through to Cassie.

What was going on here? A grown man sobbing in remorse would get through to most people. Was Cassie just a cold-hearted bitch?

Far from it. Why would Lou's tears melt Cassie's heart when his tears weren't what she needed?

What Cassie needed was to feel safe from this kind of thing ever happening again. How could she possibly feel safe when the man who had cheated on her had no clue about what his affair had really meant to her?

But weren't all those tears an indication that he knew what

he did to her? No. They were very nice, but they were like the tears of a child who knows he's done something very bad but doesn't understand exactly what he's done. All his tears said to Cassie was, "I know I've done something terrible. But I have no idea what it actually means to you. So really all I can say is that you have to forgive me because *I'm* hurting so much."

That was the message Cassie heard in Lou's tears: Lou saying, *Look at how much pain I'm in.* But what good is that to Cassie? She needs to know that he understands how much pain *she's* in. If he didn't know the cost of his betrayal to her, how could she ever trust he wouldn't do it again?

WANTING MORE. At some point in the trust-restoring process, the person who has been betrayed starts to realize that something is missing, something huge, but something a little hard to put your finger on. There's a lot of sorrow and promises to be good. But it's not really satisfying. You come away from every encounter with the other person feeling that there was something you needed and wanted that you didn't get, and it just makes you angry. Which is the last thing either of you needs.

I couldn't see this at all when I was going through it with my husband. Back then, I just knew that we'd have these painful conversations in which I poured out my heart and came away feeling very unsatisfied. He'd listen and say good things. I could tell he cared. But there was something else I was needing that we weren't coming close to hitting on.

But working over the years with people who were dealing with betrayal, I saw something very clearly: The person who was betrayed kept doing something odd. I'd done the same thing, and I had a dim feeling that it was odd when I was doing it.

We'd repeat ourselves. We'd go over and over the same litany of distress.

Julie and Steven

I remember one woman, Julie, whose husband, Steven, had cheated on her. She dragged out of him every excruciating detail of every place he'd been to with his lover. And then Julie would pour her heart out, over and over and over, about what it was like for her now to live in their neighborhood and have to avoid driving past the Starbucks where Steven and his lover had had coffee together. How she couldn't buy groceries anymore at her favorite supermarket because it was where Steven had run into his lover one day. How she couldn't go to the public library anymore because once he and his lover had met there and gone to make out in a faraway corner of the stacks.

The normal geography of her life, what was supposed to be a collection of comfortable, familiar places, had become a geography of pain. It was as if he had sown a crop of emotional landmines throughout the world she called home, making it a place of danger.

And she talked about that over and over and over.

Why?

Because she wasn't getting what she wanted. She didn't need to know that her husband felt bad. In fact, I realized one day, his feeling bad kind of pissed her off. I'd had the same experience with my husband, and it was extremely puzzling.

But with Julie I saw how all this really worked emotionally. Here's how she experienced Steven's outcries of how sorry he was. She experienced it as his way of telling her to shut up. It was as if he was saying, *Can't you see how much this hurts me? Because if you did, you'd stop going on and on about how much I'd hurt you.*

And I realized that her endless recitation of pain and anger was her way of refusing to shut up. Julie needed something else. Why would anyone repeat themselves endlessly? Because they don't feel they're being heard. If you and I are eating lunch together and I ask you to pass the salt and you do, I wouldn't have to ask again. But if you didn't pass it to me, then I'd keep asking for it.

Julie being in pain was as if she'd caught on fire. His saying he was sorry was his attempt to put it out. But her real problem wasn't that she was on fire. Her problem was that she didn't know that she'd gotten through to him.

So he had to do the very thing he dreaded most. He needed to tell her the story *from her point of view.* She needed to hear him talking about how painful it was for her to drive down the street and run into one of those emotional landmines. And he needed to do this in detail because when we've been betrayed, we experience our pain in great detail. It's all about the details.

CAN THE OTHER PERSON REALLY SEE ME AND UNDERSTAND HOW HIS BETRAYAL HAS HURT ME?

So the question you're struggling with is: "Does he really get it?" I think of this as "I need to see you seeing me." It takes account of the fact that being a good person isn't enough. Caring isn't enough. We need to know if the person who has betrayed us *really* understands how much pain they have caused us.

This is a tremendously important question. It deals with the essence of the betrayal and it gets at the heart of whether healing the mistrust is possible or not.

WHAT'S AT STAKE: The betrayer needs to understand all the ins and outs of how he's hurt you so that he can appreciate the full measure of what he's done. If he won't make an effort to see you and show you that he sees you, then you know he doesn't really care. If he *can't* see you, then you'll never feel you can trust him. Only when you see him seeing you can you have the confidence that he's not only good enough, but clued in enough to never hurt you like this again.

Back to Cassie and Lou

When we met again, at my urging Lou laid out for Cassie what his fling with the nanny had really done to Cassie. As he said it he had the look on his face of a man who is braiding a rope with which he was going to be hanged. Little did he know that what he was saying was saving their relationship.

His cheating with the nanny made Cassie wonder if he'd ever really loved her.

It made her wonder if he could ever desire her anymore: she was twenty years older than the nanny.

He'd lied about his affair. How could she trust that he hadn't lied about everything else? How would she be able to trust any-thing he said in the future?

How could she ever listen to him say affectionate things to her when she had to believe that he'd said affectionate things like that to the nanny?

How could she be at peace in their house ever again? Their house was now a place where she either knew or guessed that Lou had "done things" with the nanny. The house was now, more than anything, a place of painful memories for Cassie.

How could she face any of their friends? They either knew about the affair and pitied her or they didn't know, which meant she had a humiliating secret to protect and a reason to feel dis-tant from those friends.

By the time Lou got to the end of all this, an expression of horror beyond tears had formed on his face. Before that, it had all just been words. Heart-wrenching words, yes, like *devastated*, *betrayed*, *hurt*, but just words nonetheless. But what he'd said just now was the reality. And it was a terrible shock for Lou to see what "hurt" and "devastated" really meant. How every de-tail of Cassie's life had turned into a nightmare.

But the look on Lou's face was a great gift to Cassie. It was what she was wanting. Now, finally, she could see him really seeing her. She knew that he knew what he'd done to her, not just that her life had changed but *how*, in detail.

This is a transformational difference. The closest analogy I can think of is this. Fifty years ago, when a woman went to the hospital to give birth, her husband would stay with the other fathers in a special waiting room far from any sight or sound of actual childbirth. The fathers had no clue. They knew that something big and difficult was going on many rooms away. But the pain of childbirth was just a word to them.

This all changed when Dad joined Mom in the delivery room. Today's technology still hasn't advanced far enough for men to actually give birth themselves but because so many men are at their wives' sides throughout the whole process the women see the men seeing them. They know that their man knows what it's like. No wonder most women want their man to be there with them.

And it's the same with this part of the process toward healing broken trust. **We need to know that the other person knows the full impact of what he's done.**

Doing It Right

This ingredient is enormously healing. In many cases, it's the single most important part of the healing process.

How do you bring this ingredient into your relationship? It's actually pretty easy, if you don't screw it up. You just say something like:

> "If we're going to get past this and I'm ever going to be able to trust you again, I need to know that *you* know what a big deal this has been for me, and still is. And that means you need to listen to me when I talk about it. It's going to take a long time and you're not going to like it. Nobody wants to feel blamed and yelled at, and I know it's going to feel that way to you. And maybe part of it really will be that way. But

even if I seem like I'm blaming you, even if I really *am* blaming you, I need you to know that that's not the point of this. The point is for you just to *know*. And I'll know that you know when you show me that you know. *After I've told my story, I need to hear you telling my story.* You can't just say, 'I hear you.' You have to really say what you've seen and heard. I don't need you to defend yourself. I don't need you to talk about how sorry you are. And I don't need you to explain yourself unless I specifically ask for an explanation. I just need you to say what you've heard me say."

And *that's* how you make it possible for yourself to feel seen.

But there's something we do, both betrayer and betrayed, that prevents this vital piece of the healing process from happening. Specifically, it prevents the person who needs to see from seeing.

The Accusation/Defense Trap

Here's how it happened with Cassie and Lou.

When they got home that night, Cassie reconnected with her anger. (Let's face it, those of us who've been betrayed are always reconnecting to our anger. On the plus side, this happens less and less often with every month that goes by.) Now watch how things went haywire.

For the millionth time, Lou said he was sorry.

"You keep saying that," Cassie said. "But how can I believe it? For months you lied to my face and I never had a clue. That's what you are to me now: a liar. I just don't know how we can get past this."

In saying this, all Cassie really wanted was for Lou to see her again, just the way he had in my office. She wanted him to say something like, "I think I understand. If you didn't know I was lying then, how can you know that I'm not lying now? It's like you're living in this nightmare world where you're surrounded by the possibility of lies." That's all.

But instead of hearing Cassie's underlying plea—"I just need for you to see me because it's the only way I can come to trust that you won't hurt me again."—Lou heard the accusation. *You're a liar. You're no good. You just ruin things.*

Understandably but mistakenly, Lou did what most people in his situation do. He defended himself. Lou said, "I never meant to hurt you. I was trying to end the whole thing. I was hoping I could just put the whole thing behind me and then you'd never know and never be hurt." Poor Lou. All he wanted was not to be seen as a monster.

Poor Cassie. All she heard was this guy who'd broken her heart trying to explain to her what a great guy he was.

This is the exact opposite of what needed to happen. It's the *anti*-ingredient for healing broken trust. It's the ingredient for keeping the hurt and mistrust simmering away forever. One person shows herself and, whether she means to or not, it comes across as an accusation. The other defends his intentions. He hopes she will say, "Oh, you meant to do well! That changes everything! Everything's okay now." But what she really thinks is, "That clueless bastard. He doesn't see me. He doesn't want to see me. He doesn't really care. He's just wrapped up in wanting to look good. It's still all about him. Now I have even more evidence that I can't trust him ever again."

And then things escalate. All she wanted was to be seen, but instead he defended his intentions. Okay, fine, then she'll have to shove his nose into the mess he's made. But this more intense attempt to be seen is answered with a more strenuous defense. And the more she does things to be seen, the more he feels attacked, the more he defends himself, and the more she feels he doesn't want to see her.

Instead of her seeing him seeing her, there's a complete disconnection. You need to prevent this from happening because otherwise this all-important process of "seeing him seeing you" just won't be there.

GETTING WHAT YOU NEED. The problem is that the poor idiot who's betrayed you just doesn't understand what's really going on. He hears you being angry and upset, he hears words that sound—let's face it—pretty much like an attack, and that makes it very hard for him to hear your actual words. Remember: **The more anger in your voice, the less he hears your words. He just hears the anger. And the anger sounds like an accusation. So all he can think of to do is defend himself.**

Look, you can still be angry—although, between you and me, that makes it harder—but you need to give the other person a very strong clue about what you're really doing. Sort of like this:

> "Look, I know you feel I'm accusing you and that makes you feel that you need to defend yourself. But it's not what I'm doing and it's not what I need from you. I just need you to see me. I just need to be able to talk about the impact of what happened and have you . . . just *know* that. I don't need you to say you're sorry. I don't need you to talk about

what you meant or didn't mean to do. I just need you to show me that you understand what this was like for me."

When I work with people, I help them avoid the accusation/defense trap and stay focused on the betrayed person's need to see the other person seeing her. Every time they get off the track, I help them get back on the track. You can do that, too. It just takes patience and a watchful eye for every time you start getting into the whole accuse/defend cycle.

Just keep saying, "All I need is for you to see me," and you'll be okay. The problem isn't your anger. The problem is that there's not been a good enough frame around your anger so the other person understands what's going on.

If the person who hurt you really is a good person, he'll want to see you. If he doesn't want to see you, he's probably not a good person, and the sooner you find that out the better. Either way, you come out ahead.

9

Believing in the Relationship Again

AFTER ANGER, WHAT?

When it comes to betrayal, there's never a period when anger is 100 percent completely gone. No matter how many years go by, there's always a residue of anger, however small. A fleeting memory of the betrayal will bring a fleeting pang of anger.

But the anger itself pretty much does come to an end after about six months. It's not like suddenly the anger vanishes. It's just that you are aware that something has shifted. Anger is still there, but it's not the only thing that's there. You're aware that the relationship is there, too, and it hasn't gone away. And that's when a very important question creeps into people's minds.

Can Our Relationship Survive?

This question marks a surprising shift for many people. In the months before, while all the anger was coming out, many people realize they'd been assuming that the relationship was over. Perhaps it was over in the sense that they were planning to end it. Perhaps it was over in the sense that it would never be good again. But there's something about hanging in there during the anger stage that brings up the real possibility that the relationship can actually survive.

Maybe you haven't decided to stay but, you realize, you haven't decided to leave either. Even with all that anger. And that makes a huge difference.

WHAT'S AT STAKE: We all need hope to be able to continue putting out effort, no matter what it is we're working on. If you can't get to the point where you feel that the relationship can survive, that means you've lost hope. And so why would you put out effort? And, of course, if you don't put out any effort, you'll never restore trust and the relationship will die. But if you answer this question by having the feeling that the relationship can survive, then you'll hang in there, and that effort you put in can by itself restore trust.

Jessica and Eric

It was the office Christmas party. Everyone had had a little too much to drink—even among FBI special agents, Christmas parties can get a little wild—and Jessica was at least a couple of martinis over her limit. She was standing in a circle with some of her husband Eric's colleagues and some of the wives, too. Somehow the conversation had gotten around to Hitler of all things and someone said, "You know, that guy had only one testicle."

"Oh, yeah, I know," Jessica said, her face flushed from drinking. "And he's not the only one. Eric, too. He is mono-testicular. He's a uni-baller," she added, laughing as if this were the funniest thing in the world. It may well have been, given the way everyone was laughing their heads off.

But it wasn't so funny to Eric when some of the guys went over to him to continue this hilarious conversation. "Jessica told us about your ball situation. How does it feel to be mono-testicular?" Another guy added, "I'll say one thing for you. You've got ball." And everyone cracked up. But not Eric.

He remembered having seen Jessica with that group. He asked her what had happened and she confessed what she'd told them.

Eric was furious and also scared. He'd been about to break through to a big promotion and a prestigious assignment. And now he was just a joke. This might even be a career ender. Sure, the teasing would die down, but the mockery would always be there, just out of earshot. Every time his name came up at a meeting, someone might bring up his one-testicle status. A surefire joke. And if no one said anything, they'd be thinking it.

Eric was sure that his life was ruined. And the reason was that his wife had betrayed him. He was furious and devastated.

Was this an overreaction? We'll leave it to Eric to judge the impact of his wife's revelation on his career in the very macho FBI. He would know best. But what about the impact of it on their marriage? Couldn't he just laugh it off?

THEY NEEDED THIS LIKE A HOLE IN THE HEAD. It's important to realize something. We're more likely to get sick when we're run down. And relationships are more likely to be hit and hurt by betrayal when they're strained. That's where Jessica and Eric were. Being an FBI special agent takes its toll on a marriage. Never being able to talk about your work. Long hours. Frequent unexplained absences. The way it's hard not to bring work stress home with you. Over the years, distance and resentment had infected their marriage.

And so Eric and Jessica weren't in a good place when she shot off her mouth. Maybe that's partly why she did it. There's an element, however small, of payback in most betrayals. But whatever Jessica's motive, the two of them were in a bad place and needed this tidal wave of hurt and mistrust like a hole in the head.

HEALING'S SECRET BEGINNING. All during the time he was angry, Eric was convinced that Jessica had hurt him deliberately by broadcasting his secret. But like many women, she'd had body-image issues herself, and she felt horrified by what she'd done. As he poured his anger on her head, Jessica surprised him by being understanding and contrite. This was very effective.

Things still felt terrible, but the healing had begun. It's like you have an infection and start taking antibiotics. Are you suddenly going to be all better after you swallow the first pill? Of course not. But does that mean the medicine isn't working? Of course not. It is working. That's how working *works*. With that very first pill, real healing has started even though you initially feel just as bad as you did before.

It's the same thing with restoring trust. It stinks to go through so much anger. But that doesn't mean your relationship isn't healing. In fact a lot of healing might be happening. You just don't feel it yet.

And that's what happened with Eric and Jessica. Her being understanding and contrite actually had a huge effect on Eric's anger. It would've been more intense and lasted far longer if she had defended herself or tried to downplay the effects of what she had done. Their relationship would've been in greater jeopardy.

But still, his anger was there. And that can be a big problem as couples try to recover from a betrayal. After having done a terrible thing, Jessica was now doing all the right things and yet here was all this anger from Eric. How could she know that his anger was less than it might have been? How could she know that it would end sooner than it would have otherwise?

STAYING OFF THE ESCALATOR. So Jessica started wondering what the point was in her being so contrite. Eric's anger was making her angry. That's always a danger with anger when you're trying to heal the hurts that come from betrayal. It's the fuck-you escalator: "Fuck you." "No, fuck you." "No, fuck *you*." "*Fuck you*." "*Fuck YOU!*" "*FUCK YOU!*" Excuse my language here, but for some people, sadly, this escalator is their lives, and it can go on for years, or forever.

Somehow, though, Jessica dredged up enough wisdom to prevent her from piling her anger onto Eric's. And that did a wonderful thing. It made it possible for this hurt, wounded man to catch glimpses of the woman he'd liked and loved before this terrible incident.

And so, sooner than many people in his situation, though far later than Jessica would have liked, Eric quietly realized that their relationship would survive. There are no trumpet fanfares when this happens. It's like when your headache goes away. You never know the moment when it passes. You just realize that for some time now it's been gone.

There he was with the realization that he hadn't left in spite of all the times he'd thought of leaving. There he was thinking he wasn't going to leave either. It's not the same as knowing you're going to stay. It's just the knowledge that you're not ending it yet.

A STEP TOWARD TRUST. This is a good moment, a healthy moment. It's an important step in restoring trust and healing the relationship. But it's not necessarily a happy moment. After all, you've been terribly hurt and you're still very vulnerable. And yet now you see yourself maybe staying.

A lot of people hate themselves for thinking of staying like this, women particularly. Perhaps they feel that if they were braver they would choose to leave. Sometimes staying feels like being beaten down emotionally. It's like having nowhere to go. Nothing better to do. It can sometimes feel like being trapped.

It's painful to feel this way, but we need to be realistic. What did you think the first hints of wanting to recommit to this relationship would feel like? Wild enthusiasm? Hardly. At best, at this stage, you're going to be incredibly wary about wading back in. How else would you feel about a relationship in which you've gotten so badly hurt?

But this wariness isn't a sign that you're making a mistake in thinking you just might be able to hang in there. It's a sign that you've been hurt. Which is not news. What is news, big news, is that **in spite of being hurt, in spite of being wary, your heart is open to the possibility that your broken trust can heal and that your relationship can be made new.**

But, of course, you're not out of the woods yet.

SUSTAINABLE TRUST

When Jessica realized that Eric's anger had died down, when she saw that his tone toward her was more businesslike or even normal or even, in some cases, friendly, she was delighted. She felt she could breathe again. "Ahh," she thought, "he's letting go of this."

But *that's* the danger here. Everyone thinks it's the beginning of the final resolution when you start thinking the relationship can survive. "We're out of the woods now," people think. But that's not what's going on at all. It's not the new beginning following the end. It's not even the end of the beginning. It's the beginning of the beginning.

And that's because only now have Jessica and Eric begun to leave crazyland. The anger that threatened to consume them, and did in fact blind them, has receded enough so that the survival of the relationship seems possible. Only now can trust begin to be restored, and there's a lot of work to do.

But who wants to do that work? Both Jessica *and* Eric were sick of his anger. Sometimes people who've been betrayed, like Eric, decide at this point to hide their mistrust. Sometimes people who've done the betraying, like Jessica, decide not to see the mistrust. The temptation is for Jessica, who's emotionally exhausted, to say, "Look, sweetie, I'm really, really sorry for what I did to you. I'll never, ever do anything like that again. Can we just put all this behind us?"

And then Eric, exhausted himself, is, oh-so-tempted to say, "Sure."

What a mistake. The baby of healing has just been born and now everyone strangles it in the crib.

DON'T JUST STAND THERE. DO SOMETHING. Again, the need for safety has trumped the need for trust. The anger had scared everybody and to feel safe both people are tempted to run away from anger, particularly now that the decision to stay has been made. But this won't build trust. It will drive the mistrust underground where it never changes, never heals. Politeness and a neutral atmosphere might feel safe, but they are no substitute for trust. All they do is promote distance, so the couple end up like two people in separate life rafts in the middle of the ocean, and as the seas roll and the wind blows they just drift farther and farther away from each other.

And so the mistake here is doing nothing. The mistake is being so glad the anger's died down a little, so glad that the threat of leaving is less ominous, that you want to pretend that everything is okay.

There's a part of everyone that wants to do this because by this point we're so exhausted. The way I felt when I was at this point was, fine, I won't be angry, I'll just be polite from now on. But I could feel the danger. It suddenly felt as though I was looking at my husband through the wrong end of a telescope, and he seemed a hundred miles away. And I had this sense that if we stayed distant and didn't deal with anything, the craziness might seem to be gone, but we would never be close again. When you're exhausted, that can, if only for a moment, seem like a good deal. But it isn't.

So if you've been betrayed and you're scared and exhausted from all the anger that's come out from both of you and you suddenly feel that possibility of committing to each other again and there's a part of you that just wants to let things ride, DON'T. Instead, you need to say to the other person something like, "Look, we've been through hell. And I know we're both feeling burned out. But we still have a real problem. Trust was seriously damaged. Now that we can begin to talk to each other without going nuts, we have to start repairing that damage."

And how do you do that exactly? Most people don't have a clue. All we know how to do is act so angry and menacing that, we hope, the other person will be scared to hurt us again. But while this gives us the illusion of feeling safe, it damages the relationship and does nothing to promote trust.

But I've got some good news for you. You're on the verge of actually doing what you need to do to restore trust if you just hang in there for what comes next.

10

So This Will Never
Happen Again

Jess and Jenny

Jess and Jenny had been best friends since high school. They
went to the same state college and, after dating other people for
a couple of years, were astounded to find themselves falling
madly in love with each other after so many years of friendship.
A year after college they were married. By the time they reached
middle age, their lives were busy and complicated but they still
thought of each other as best friends as well as lovers. They both
believed they could count on the other to be there for them no
matter what. And so it had seemed throughout all their ups and
downs.

But something changed all that. Jenny got breast cancer. I
won't keep you in suspense: she eventually got better and has
been fine for the last seven years. But for a while it was scary.

It was also surprisingly scary for Jess. The thought of cancer touching so close to home freaked him out. He couldn't think of what to say or do. So Jess pulled away from Jenny. She just couldn't get him to talk with her much about what she was going through. Jess felt terribly guilty because he knew he should be there for his wife. But he just couldn't.

Jenny felt abandoned and betrayed. Of all the times to be abandoned by your spouse! It's like your husband walking out on you when you're pregnant. Naturally, as with all betrayals, the whole world now looked different to Jenny. The cancer itself had been a betrayal: Every time something serious and scary goes wrong with our bodies, we feel deeply let down. And when you pile one betrayal on top of another, the effects just multiply. As Jenny put it, "I can't trust my body. I can't trust my husband. Who can I trust?"

Jenny developed a suspicious, angry relationship with her doctors and her husband. She was, in effect, pushing them away, even though that wasn't her intention. But in pushing them away she gave herself even more reason to be mistrustful.

Eventually Jess heard that the treatments were taking hold and that Jenny was starting to do better. Overcome with relief and guilt, knowing he'd done a terrible thing, Jess started reaching out again to Jenny.

NOT MAKING THINGS WORSE. Jess guessed he was in for it and he was right. For a long time Jenny just wouldn't respond to Jess, but eventually she just let him have it. Jess got the full brunt of Jenny's anger. Jenny just needed to howl. At one point Jenny came close to slapping Jess.

But Jess did something—the *key* thing—to healing the broken trust. *He didn't make things worse.* That's it. Things will get better if you don't make them worse. And Jess had a lot of opportunities to make things worse. In her anger Jenny said a lot of things that weren't true or fair. It feels like you're being assaulted when you're on the receiving end of that kind of anger.

But instead of defending himself or attacking back, Jess hung in there, intuiting that Jenny just needed to get her anger out. And boy, did Jenny get it out! She roared like a lion. She let her anger flow like red-hot lava. She needed to. She was just trying to make herself feel safe. But this is incredibly dangerous because at any moment Jess could've said, "The hell with you. I don't need this."

But thank God Jess hung in there all the way through to the point—invisible to Jess—when Jenny realized that she wasn't breaking off their relationship.

CAN WE REPAIR THE PROBLEM THAT GOT US INTO TROUBLE IN THE FIRST PLACE? So Jess stuck it out and hung in there through the period Jenny was asking herself this question: *Can we repair the problem that got us into trouble in the first place?* This is not just testing. Something actually has to be accomplished here. Things have to get better.

This is different from mere anger. There's a lot more than just yelling. There are questions, demands for explanations. There are criticisms. There's an insistence that the other person do different things. If anger was a way to give yourself the illusion that you're safe, this is an opportunity to create real safety, and real trust in the bargain.

Jenny, for example, told Jess that she needed Jess to come with her to a cancer survivors' support group. Talk about torture! Jess hadn't been able to handle his wife getting sick. How would he ever handle a roomful of cancer-stricken strangers? But by going with her nonetheless, Jess was solving a problem that had caused the original betrayal.

So can they make the relationship better? This is a tremendously important question. It deals with the essence of the betrayal and it gets at the heart of whether healing the mistrust is possible or not.

WHAT'S AT STAKE: **All you have to do is figure out what led to the betrayal and deal with it. If you can't do that, not only will you never feel safe, you'll never *be* safe. But if you can make things in your relationship better in a way that makes betrayal less likely, that makes all the difference. It's like having water come into your house, figuring out where the leak in your roof is, and then fixing that leak. Then you can both feel safe and be safe. And trust can come alive again.**

MAKING THINGS GOOD ENOUGH

When two people get to this point in the process of healing broken trust, they have a very specific problem to solve. Yes, the betrayer is sorry. Yes, he's so sorry he's willing to be raked over the coals. Yes, the person who's been betrayed can imagine staying in the relationship. Yes, the craziness has died down to the point where the two people can talk. Yes, there's hope.

The problem, though, is, what's really been solved? Not much, actually.

Whatever led up to the betrayal is still there. Let's say I betrayed you by lying to you. Okay. But after I'd proved to you that I was really sorry and that I was willing to hang in there . . . so what? That's a beginning, but can you really trust that I won't lie again? There was a reason why I lied in the first place. Maybe the reason was in me. Some fear, or some lack of skill. But maybe the reason had something to do with you: maybe you were doing something that made it hard for me to be honest.

Let's go back to Jess and Jenny. Jenny was feeling very insecure. Jess had abandoned her at her moment of greatest need. But Jess was feeling insecure, too. Would Jess be able to step up? Or would he let his wife down again?

They have to figure all this out and fix it, and the question we're facing here is, *Can we do this?*

REAL SOLUTIONS, REAL SAFETY, REAL TRUST

Before we get into this, let me make something perfectly clear. **It's not your fault that you were betrayed. Period.** A betrayal is like a mugging. It's not your fault that you were mugged either. So there's nothing anyone could ever point to and say *that* justifies your being betrayed.

Are we clear on that? Good.

Rebuilding trust means preventing the possibility of betrayal in the future. And *that* means looking to see if there are any underlying problems that somehow, in part, led to the betrayal.

Some of these problems could be issues your partner needs to deal with. For example, maybe your partner is someone who hates confrontation. Now that's a pretty common problem for someone to have. But hating confrontation means he won't want to deal with you. Which means he's going to tend to go behind your back to deal with things. Which could easily lead to betrayal.

And—sorry, honey, but I have to say it—some of these problems could be issues you need to deal with. Again, not that it's your fault that you were betrayed, but still maybe there are things you can do to make it less likely that betrayal happens in the future.

Let me tell you about what happened with me.

THAT DAMNED EMOTIONAL AFFAIR AGAIN. I've mentioned that my husband had this emotional affair. He shouldn't have done that. Nothing I'd done justified his doing that. But here comes the "but." I had in fact made it far too easy for him to go off and have an emotional affair.

Let me spell out my contribution to our disaster. I was very busy. I was very impatient. I was very critical of him. I was very unsupportive when my husband was going through a difficult time himself. Somehow, I had withdrawn from him. And he felt it very keenly. The mistake I made was something like what I wrote about in my book *The Weekend Marriage*: busy and stressed out, I acted as if I could put my husband and our relationship on a back shelf where it would just sit there like a package of Twinkies and never get stale or go sour.

My husband's part in the problem was that he didn't know

how to get my attention and let me know what he needed and how we were going off the rails. My part in the problem was that I ignored his needs and sent us off the rails.

Would he have had that emotional affair if I'd been warmer, more supportive, and more attentive? Who knows. But I think it would have been a hell of a lot less likely. The odds are that it wouldn't have happened.

I wouldn't dream of asking you and the other person to try to figure out the underlying problem until things have calmed down emotionally. You will need to be in a place where you can have normal conversations about normal things. A place where you are at least beginning to feel that the other person does see how difficult this has all been for you.

And when you find yourselves in this somewhat better place, that's when you need to have the conversation. It's not a "problem" conversation. Who wants that! It's a *prevention* conversation. Just say something like,

> "I'd like to prevent this from ever happening again. This has nothing to do with our blaming each other. No blame, okay? But let's see if we can figure out if there isn't something about you and about me that led to this happening. Please tell me if there's anything I did that somehow led to your doing what you did. And then let's talk a bit to see if there's anything I can help you with so you don't ever have to do anything like that again."

This is a problem-identifying and problem-solving conversation. If you can't do it without blowing up at each other, then you need to find a professional who can help you. Many couples can do this on their own if they just wait until the worst of the anger has died down. For some couples it's a little harder.

Ryan and Dawn

As is usually the case, there were already a number of problems in their relationship by the time Dawn discovered that Ryan had cheated on her. When they were just going out, Ryan had gotten the impression that Dawn was a fun-loving, take-it-easy kind of gal. Once they got married, though, Ryan thought a different Dawn came out—an ambitious, hard-working, highly organized person. Dawn said she's always been the same person and never tried to hide her personality, but Ryan hadn't ever seen that side of her. He was shocked and upset at the growing realization that his fun gal had turned into a tough taskmaster.

Ryan hadn't been looking for an affair but three years into his marriage he was ripe for the plucking by any woman who showed the promise of affection.

And he found her. It seems like one of those sad ironies of life that married people hungry for affection too often find someone outside their marriage than in it. And that's how it worked out for Ryan.

Of course the wheels of fate keep turning, and before long they turned as they inevitably do toward revealing Ryan's secret. Dawn was horrified and furious. How *dare* he do this to her! They went through a long period of hell, but in the end Dawn decided that she wasn't ready to end this marriage. And Ryan genuinely wanted to heal things.

They made a lot of progress, but at one point things fell apart.

To forgive Ryan, Dawn needed to see that Ryan understood what had led him to make the terrible decision to have an affair. "Why didn't you just come to me?" she said. "We could have figured something out."

But Ryan saw things completely differently. "The problem wasn't that I didn't deal with you. The problem was that I *couldn't* deal with you. I tried to talk to you about what was going on. About what was bothering me. And you just made me feel bad. You made me feel there was something wrong with me because I couldn't deal with the fact that you were so busy and distracted and couldn't show me any affection."

Dawn blew up. "So you're saying it's my fault you had an affair? That's insane! That's the craziest thing I ever heard!"

And on they went, each blaming the other for what had happened.

Blame is a fundamental mistake people make in trying to find forgiveness and restore trust.

THE MAGIC PILL. I've got a pill for you, just one pill, that will make it possible for you to let go of blame and find forgiveness. It's an extremely effective pill. There's just one thing: It's a big pill to swallow. But you can swallow it, and if you do, you'll be on your way.

The pill is this: *Whenever there's been a betrayal there are problems on both sides and both people need to take responsibility for the part they've played.*

I know exactly what you're thinking. Dawn thought the same thing, and she said it: "It's *not* my fault that that fucking bastard cheated on me. All he had to do was keep it zipped. No one forced him to do it."

I totally agree. In the world of moral judgments, some people are far more culpable than others. Out of all the betrayals I've seen in my work—and they're countless—no one was ever forced into betraying the other person.

THE WORLD WHERE TRUST-BUILDING HAPPENS

There's another world, though, and it's the one I want to focus on. It's the real, practical world where healing happens. It's not the world of whose fault it is that the bridge collapsed. It's the world of repairing that bridge.

And the pill you need to swallow, the pill that will make all the difference, is that **If you can come together in the spirit of understanding that you both contributed to what happened and there are things you both need to work on to repair the relationship, then you will heal the problems in your relationship and, ultimately, be in a position to restore trust.**

In principle, it's not really all that hard. You come together and one of you says, "My part in what happened is . . . ," and then you discuss that.

Then the other says, "My part in what happened is . . ." and you go on to discuss that.

And *please*, do not even *begin* to talk about whose part was bigger. That's a moral judgment discussion and it will not bring about healing. The healing discussion is when you both take responsibility for the part each of you played and leave it at that.

I know how these discussions go. The other person is going to be more than helpful when it comes to pointing to things that contribute to your part in what happened. And you will be ready, willing, and able to say what the other person's part is in what happened.

You can see where this might end up. A blame jamboree. There's a thin line between your healthfully pointing out my role in what happened and your blaming me for what happened.

So what is that difference? How do you do this without falling into the blame game? The solution is this: forget your dream of the other person saying things so nicely, so helpfully that there's no hint of blame in it. Instead, the solution that works best is *to just not hear the blame.* It might be there, or it might not be there, but either way you won't hear it.

You'll just hear what the other person says as a fact. It might be a fact stated with anger and resentment, but to them it's a fact nonetheless.

ON NOT HEARING BLAME. For example, Dawn would have heard Ryan say, "It was like you'd tossed me aside. You were too busy for me and what made it worse is that you seemed to have lost interest in me. The only interest you had in me was in pointing out my flaws."

If Dawn's smart, she will *not* say, "That's not true and it's not fair. I never meant to push you aside. I did my best. But I was working so hard. What did you want from me . . ."

Oy. When I hear someone say something like that in therapy I think it's such a mistake. It's not that what Dawn is saying isn't true; she's telling the truth about her life and her feelings. But this is not a court of law where we're trying to establish the truth. This is a problem-solving session. Ryan was saying what was missing for him. At this moment it doesn't matter what

Dawn's intentions were or whether or not she was more loving than Ryan thinks she was. Ryan is simply saying that, "Your part in what happened is that you weren't there for me." And since Dawn now knows that this is Ryan's reality and that's what he needs, all she has to say is, "I hear that you need me to be more affectionate from now on. What can I do to show you that?" In the world of problem-solving, that would be a perfect response.

That's the key to problem solving without blame: You refuse to hear blame. You just hear a need. And you don't judge that need nor do you try to justify yourself for whether or not you've tried to meet that need. You hear the need and talk about trying to meet it.

STAYING OUT OF TROUBLE

Let's talk about a couple of ways people get in trouble trying to avoid the blame game.

Self-righteousness

This is when one of you basically says "I'm right and you can't possibly be right." That's what was going on with Dawn and Ryan . . . Dawn was trying to win an imaginary case in front of an imaginary judge.

Remember: we're not doing judgment here. We're doing problem-solving.

So if you say you need me to be more affectionate, well, then, that's what you need. We just have to figure out what you mean by "be more affectionate" and what I can do to give you that.

After Ryan and Dawn tussled and tangled for a while, it turned out that when Ryan said he needed Dawn to be more affectionate he meant, "Touch me and hug me and kiss me and, once in a while, initiate lovemaking." And that, Dawn realized, was very doable.

Impatience

It can be very hard for us to sit still through the process of working out meeting another's needs.

It would be so much easier if our relationships were like McDonald's. Here's the deal about McDonald's: They accept what you need as long as you accept what they have to offer. Every time you walk in and say, I'd like a Big Mac, they give it to you. They don't question your need. They don't say, "Hey, I gave you a Big Mac yesterday and now you want another?" They don't complain about how hard it is to give you a Big Mac. They just give it to you.

You, for your part, know the deal. You don't ask for fried squid. You don't ask for beef Wellington. You don't ask if they can charcoal broil your Big Mac.

It's a great relationship because it's based on total acceptance.

Now you can see why we get so impatient with each other when it comes to meeting each other's needs. We don't fully accept what one needs and what the other has to offer. To be more specific, I don't accept what you need and you don't accept that I have trouble giving it to you.

That's where impatience comes in. It's really a mixture of frustration, hunger, and disbelief. Something that should be easy, we feel, turns out to be really hard. Instead of it being like walking into McDonald's wanting a Big Mac, it's like walking into an unknown restaurant where the chef is very busy and you don't know what he can make for you, nor does he know what you really want.

The solution to impatience is appropriate expectations. If you know there's going to be a lot of traffic driving to work on a Monday morning, with a lot of delays, then you'll leave early and allow for that. That way your expectations will be in line with reality. And it works the same way when it comes to problem-solving. You need to accept the following:

- You will say things that seem perfectly clear to you and yet the other person won't understand.

- You will ask for something that seems perfectly reasonable to you and yet the other person will raise difficulties about providing it.

- You will start out from a very simple place and yet before you know it things will get incredibly tangled up.

- You will describe something that seems quite obvious and yet the other person will astound you by saying you're totally wrong.

These things will happen. If you can accept that and patiently deal with each one of these snafus, you will solve your problems.

Let me make the whole thing really simple. Something bad happened and one of you betrayed the other. There are many possible explanations for what happened. But a very useful explanation is that there were things you needed from each other that you weren't getting that led to what happened. If you'd gotten those things, the betrayal would have been less likely to happen.

But if you can find a way to give each other those things now, a similar betrayal will be less likely to happen in the future. If you can't find a way to give each other what you need—to even listen to each other talk about what you need—then you should probably look at whether it even makes sense for the two of you to be together.

But if you can address the underlying problem that led to the betrayal, even if you don't completely solve it, then you've almost completed the process of restoring trust.

THE TOP SIX SOLUTIONS THAT PREVENT BETRAYAL

Some people don't have a lot of experience talking about their problems in a constructive way. There may be fighting and blaming, but not a lot of good problem identifying.

So to help you, here's my list of the top six solutions one or both people need to prevent betrayal:

1. Learn to listen.
We're all so full of grievances and stress and unmet needs—don't get me started on my own!—that most of us have a hard time listening to the other person in a way that makes him feel heard. We interrupt. We say, "Yes, but . . ." and then launch into our own point of view. We criticize. We minimize. We blame. We feel blamed.

All of this prevents listening from happening. And, you see, if you don't feel that I'm really listening to you, then you won't feel you can deal with me or even talk to me. So you're that much more likely to just go off and do whatever the hell you want. And then I'll feel betrayed.

Or maybe it's because you can't listen to me that you don't understand where I'm coming from and what I need. And so you go off and do whatever you want and I feel betrayed.

And here's a big, big tip: Listening means hearing. And you show you've heard by reflecting back what you've heard. That means doing anything from repeating the same words to asking questions that show you were paying attention to offering solutions that show that you get what the other person was saying.

It's so clear: more listening, less betrayal.

2. Make each other feel the other matters.

This is what a relationship *is*: two people signaling that they matter to each other in some special way, as friends, lovers, relatives, business partners, you name it. You don't need to matter to each other *more than* your relationship requires—business partners are not going to send Valentine's Day cards to each other—but you do have to feel that you matter to each other *as much as* your relationship requires.

Ah, but that's so often easier said than done. Particularly in intimate relationships, we're so often so busy, so distracted, so stressed out that we feel we're running on empty. How can I make you feel you matter to me when I'm feeling I'm just putting out and not getting much back?

I realize it's hard. Harder now than ever. But the fact remains: If I don't make you feel that you matter to me, that just loosens the bonds between us. And you're that much more likely to go off and do something that will make me feel betrayed. You may very well not even see it as a betrayal, because if you don't matter to me, then what difference does it make what you do?

And this is sad, because it's so easy to make someone feel they matter. For one thing, listening helps. (We just talked about that!) Making time for each other. Occasionally doing something nice. Reaching out now and then.

It's all about the little things.

3. Be fair.

"It's just not fair that I come home from work and you've been home for an hour already from your job and you haven't lifted a finger to get dinner started."

Or, "It's just not fair that you make so much more money than I do and yet you expect me to pay for every little thing fifty-fifty."

Or, "It's just not fair that I have to spend hours and hours listening to you talk about your problems, but whenever I talk about my problems you barely show any interest."

We all have things like these in our relationships. They lead to disappointment and resentment and anger and fights and distance and revenge and . . . well, I don't have to tell you. All I can say is that there's no relationship in the world where everything is perfectly fair. But if things get out of whack to the point where one of you is feeling resentment, then that means you've just hopped on the train that's going to take you to downtown Betrayalville.

But I'll tell you a secret. Things don't have to be perfectly fair to eliminate resentment from a relationship. It's so often the case that even if things are a little unfair you won't feel much resentment as long as you feel that you've been heard and the other person understands and at least tries to make things more balanced.

It's not perfect fairness but a real attempt at showing caring that begins to ease resentment.

4. Learn how to make decisions together.

It's all very nice to be in a relationship with someone where you both like exactly the same things. You want a circular dining room table and so does he. Wow! It's so easy.

That's a very nice kind of compatibility to have, but, let's face it, no two people are going to like the same things in every single area. So there's another kind of compatibility that's even more important: being able to decide together what you're going to do when you don't start out wanting the same thing.

If you and the other person both want to eat Italian food for dinner, well, that's easy. But if you want Italian and the other wants Chinese, then what do you do? In far too many relationships, what you do is this: one of you just decides on your own that it's easier to go along with the other person than to actually work out a good solution that makes both of you happy. In other words, you decide by not deciding. You just accommodate.

Which too often becomes one-sided. Which leads to unfairness. Which leads to resentment. Which takes us back to Betrayalville.

Here, too, I have a secret for you. Actually deciding—as opposed to one of you just accommodating—rarely takes more than five minutes. *Five* minutes! That's the real difference between two people who make good decisions together and two people who don't.

How do you use those five minutes? There are a number of different tactics that are all effective in making a decision together so that the process seems fair and the outcome is good.

TACTIC #1: Use your numbers. This works very often, and it's really fast. So you can't agree on something. Then each of you think of a number from 1 to 10 that represents how important your choice is to you. One means you barely don't care and ten means you want it as much as you've ever wanted anything. Then you tell each other your numbers. The person with the highest number wins.

TACTIC #2: Taking turns. What if your numbers are the same or you just don't want to use your numbers? Flip a coin. Whoever wins this time gets their choice, then you take turns and the other person gets to choose next time. Again, it's fast and fair.

TACTIC #3: "This is important to me because . . ." I've noticed that couples very often get stuck making a decision because they don't understand why each other's choices are important to them. So before you get into a big ugly argument, each of you says why you want what you want. Talk about what it really means to you.

TACTIC #4: Kicking it around. I've seen it over and over: two people get polarized before they've ever really talked about their options. Okay, so one of you wants the white couch and the other wants two leather club chairs. Fine. But before you get locked in, just sit down and kick around the whole furniture-buying thing. Why are you buying this stuff now? What are you hoping to get out of it? What are some other options you've never even talked about before? Often when people kick around the options before they get locked in, they make better choices without the stress.

Invest the time in using one of these tactics. We're only talking about five lousy minutes. But the payoff is enormous. Not only will your relationship be better—and freer from the threat of betrayal—but your whole life will work better. Five minutes! It's well worth it.

5. Don't belittle.

Aretha Franklin spelled it out for us in case we missed the point. R-E-S-P-E-C-T. And is that too much to ask for?

It really isn't. All anyone ever wants is to be treated as if they're not stupid, not ignorant, not crazy, and not unimportant. It's all I want. What about you? We don't need for the other person to kiss our ass. We just don't want anyone to belittle us.

Sure, some putdowns are intended. And they can really hurt. But a bigger problem is unintended putdowns. I did this to my husband just a few minutes ago. We were talking about something we needed to buy and I "explained" something about the way it works. If I'd thought for a second, I would've realized that of course he knew that already. By "explaining" it to him, I was treating him as if he were both ignorant and stupid. And he quite rightly bristled.

Now one incident like this doesn't matter much in the grand scheme of things. But too often there's a constant diet of it.

So how do you solve this problem? Here's what *not* to do. Don't put the other person down for putting you down. Instead, say something like, "Let's just point out to each other whenever one of us says something that makes the other feel small. We won't argue about it. Or explain it, or defend it. It'll just be like, 'Oh, so it made you feel belittled when I said that? Good feedback.'"

That's all there is to it. If the two of you have good will toward each other, then weeding out these little comments that make each other feel small will make a huge difference. And if you're not making each other feel small, there won't be anger and resentment which, of course, lead to betrayal.

It will lead instead to *anti-betrayal*. The opposite of betrayal. And what's that? Well, if betrayal is doing something bad to the other person behind their back, then anti-betrayal is doing something good for the other person to her face. That's the kind of relationship I want. Where I anti-betray you and you anti-betray me. Wouldn't that be great?

6. Don't be controlling.

We human beings hate being controlled and do everything we can to resist it. This is an incredibly important cause of betrayal. The more you try to control me, the more likely it is that I'm going to do something to break out of the bounds you've set, whether I do so accidently or deliberately.

The tragedy here is that one person's controlling behavior is another person's need. This even held true for Jess and Jenny.

Jenny just needed Jess to be there for her while she was dealing with her cancer. Jess, right or wrong, experienced this as controlling behavior and felt he needed to break free.

I understand the difficulty. Telling someone to stop being so controlling is like telling someone to stop having their needs. Of course I'm not telling you to not have your needs; I'm just telling you to be smart. If your needs are going to be experienced by the other person as control, it doesn't mean you have to throw your needs overboard. It just means you have to have a conversation.

If you do this the right way, a seeming miracle can happen. If I flatly present a need to you, you're going to hear it as a demand and you're going to feel controlled. So that's the wrong way. Here's the way that works. I present my need to you as part of a conversation, so it becomes a kind of negotiation. If you do this the right way, a seeming miracle can happen.

Suppose, Jenny had said to Jess, "I got some really bad news. It turns out that I have cancer. I know that freaks a lot of people out and makes them terribly uncomfortable. But I really need your support now. What can I do so that it's more comfortable for you to listen to me talk about it?"

This makes it much more likely that Jenny won't feel controlled and will feel able to be there for her friend. And that is a kind of miracle.

There are some forms of control that can be very important to watch out for while people are trying to restore trust in a relationship.

HYPERVIGILANCE CAN RESULT IN HYPER-HIDING. Most people like a little bit of privacy. It's not that they're doing anything wrong. It's just that they may not want to be seen doing what they're doing. For example, a lot of the things I buy I buy online. There's nothing wrong with what I buy; if a list of every single thing I bought online last year were to appear on the front page of the *New York Times*, it wouldn't cause me a moment's embarrassment. Still, if I felt that my husband were spying on me and monitoring my online spending habits, even though I only use my own money, it would make me uncomfortable. I don't really know why. It just would. So if I felt he was snooping into my online purchases, I'd start hiding.

It's just the way people work. If one person snoops, the other's going to hide. Unfortunately, snooping is often a big part of the aftermath of betrayal: *you hurt me so much that in order for me to feel safe I need to keep tabs on you.*

And this goes much further than just snooping. Hypervigilance can extend everywhere. After my husband's emotional affair I kept asking him what he was thinking about. Of course I wanted to know if he was thinking about *her*. And of course by doing this I was opening a huge can of worms.

Like most people, my husband had a reluctance to sharing every single thought. Not because his thoughts were evil. But sometimes because they were silly or meaningless or he just needed them to be private. By trying to probe into his thoughts to know him better, I ended up pushing him further away.

I'd have done much better to say something like, "Look, I still feel scared and vulnerable, and it would help me feel safe if you were more open with me. I'll try not to constantly bug you and probe, but if you could be more open with me I'd really appreciate it and I promise not to judge and I'll do my best to make you glad you shared."

So if you're at a point where you just have to snoop and push and probe, share that need and then back off. If you can't do that, well, realize that you might actually end up getting less than you had before. In a way, snooping is like cheating. If you don't get caught, it looks like there's no harm done. But if you do get caught—and people almost always do—all hell breaks loose. The damage that results is rarely worth it.

OVERCONTROLLING BEHAVIOR PROVOKES REBELLION. You have to be particularly careful about controlling behavior during the trust-healing process. When Jess was trying to patch things up with Jenny, at one point Jenny went too far and almost ruined everything. She not only wanted Jess to go to cancer survivor support group meetings, she started dictating to Jess which meetings he had to go to. That was just too much for Jess. Now his wife just seemed like a control freak. Jess refused to allow this level of control and fortunately Jenny backed down.

But many people, particularly married people, don't back down. They're so hurt and scared and angry that they feel they need all the control they could possibly get. What can I say? If the need you have for control goes way over the amount of control your partner is willing to put up with, then you might have a big problem. All I can suggest is that you ask yourself some questions:

- Can you actually control the thing you're trying to control? One woman, for example, told her husband not to talk to his ex. They had many huge battles over this. But in the end, how could she control this situation? Her husband could talk to his ex at work whenever he wanted and no one would know the difference.

- If you did control it, would it give you what you needed? Really think about this. Is control what you need? Wouldn't you rather not have control and just see what the other person does on his own? Control, assuming you can even get it, might make you feel safe, but it won't help you trust the other person one little bit.

On the other hand, if you don't try to control the other person, that kind of gives you a win/win. Either he shows that, nope, he can't be trusted. In which case you know the truth, and better to know it now than later. Or he shows that he can be trusted. And then you have something much better than safety.

You might be thinking: *I know what he's going to do if I don't control him and it ain't pretty.* All right, then, let me see if I can understand what you're saying. You're either saying this person is thoughtless and irresponsible, but you want him in your life anyway. Or you're saying that when it comes to matters very important to you, this person has radically different values, but you want him in your life anyway.

Am I missing something? Why do you want this person in your life? In my experience, when you *have* to control someone who's close to you—which is usually exhausting—there's a good case to be made that the relationship just isn't worth it.

If you have to control the other person, what have you really gotten for yourself? Think about it, okay?

A NOTE ON PROBLEM SOLVING

Earlier, I said that if you can't solve the underlying problems, it makes sense to think about whether you should go forward with the relationship. I think that was a little stark. I need to say more.

Let's face it, it's really hard for couples to solve their problems. That's just the way it is. Some issues can be worked out easily. There are other areas where you can't seem to make any progress no matter how hard you try.

But if all you've done is try to solve your problems on your own that does *not* mean you should throw in the towel. Far from it. It means that it's time to get professional help. And that means going to work with a good couples therapist, which can make all the difference. The technology for helping couples today is amazing. I know that on television we see all these lame therapists who just sit around listening to people complain about their problems. Maybe that's good for comedy or drama. But in real life, good therapists get in there and actually help uncover solutions to problems people thought could never be solved. In fact, state-of-the-art couples therapy is one of the most effective forms of clinical intervention there is for any problem.

You cannot say that you're unable to solve your problems unless a good therapist has proven unable to help you solve your problems.

You may not need that. There are plenty of tools for doing this on your own here. There are many more tools in my book *Our Love Is Too Good to Feel So Bad*. But if that's not enough, don't worry. It's normal to need professional help. To need it and not get it is a big mistake.

So HOW, THEN, do you get an answer to that question: Can we make things safer and better in our relationship? If you just use the tools I've given you in this chapter, you'll be all set. Remember, things don't become safer and better because both people become perfect. Things become safer and better because both people work together to try to achieve these important results. It's that trying that makes all the difference, and that immediately puts you in the top 10 percent of all relationships.

11

Forgiveness and Beyond

A ND THEN THERE'S the sixth and last question people who've been betrayed ask: *Can I forgive him?* It's all too easy to let this question slide. You've made a lot of progress and solved a lot of problems. You're back in the relationship, more or less. So why not just forget about the whole forgiveness thing?

Because that would be a huge mistake.

WHAT'S AT STAKE: Forgiveness isn't just the cherry on top of the sundae of reconciliation. It's absolutely essential. Without forgiveness, the hurt and anger never really end. What's more, you can't trust someone you don't forgive and, just as important, you can't trust someone who doesn't forgive you. But when you forgive, along with everything else you've

**done, you've rooted out every bit of infection. Trust can be
restored and the relationship can thrive again.**

There's just one thing, though. It's hard to believe that you
can forgive if you don't know how to forgive.

I can't tell you how many times I've had the following conversation with a patient:

"Have you forgiven him yet?"

"No."

"So tell me: What is this forgiveness that you haven't found
yet?"

"I don't know."

And you see, that's the thing. It's not that it's so hard to forgive; it's that we don't have a clear sense of what forgiveness is.
It would be like you asking me to help you find something you'd
lost, but you couldn't say exactly what it was that you'd lost. I
know how to look for a gold earring or a set of keys. I don't know
how to look for . . . something undefined.

So what exactly is this forgiveness that some of us have such
trouble finding? Let me tell you a story.

Tim's story

Tim, a high school senior, was driving down a two-lane high-
way with some friends. Up ahead he saw some young people
riding their bicycles. Tim was driving at a moderate speed and
positioned himself to give the bicyclists a wide berth. When he
was almost even with them, one of the bicyclists suddenly

swerved left and rode her bike right out into the road in front of him. It was horrifying and inexplicable. Tim didn't even have time to put on his brakes until after he hit her.

The police and ambulance came and the young woman was taken to the hospital, where she soon died. She was sixteen, and she went to Tim's high school. He knew her. And he'd killed her. The police questioned a number of witnesses including drivers who were driving on the other side of the road and had seen the accident, as well as the young girl's friends who were with her and also the people in Tim's car. Without exception they all said that the young woman had veered into the road in a way that probably made it impossible for Tim to have done anything to prevent the accident.

The police didn't press charges. But they went even further. The chief of police in that small community made a statement that appeared on the front page of the local paper in which he said that Tim was completely without fault in that accident.

But when Tim went back to school he found that there were people who couldn't forgive him, particularly the young woman's friends. Yes, Tim had been found officially innocent. And yet he'd killed her. How can you forgive that?

A week later, Tim went to the girl's funeral. He hadn't wanted to go. He'd been completely devastated by what had happened. But his father urged him to go, and he went.

While Tim was standing looking at the casket a funeral director materialized at his side and led him into a small room where the girl's parents were. Of all people, they were the very last Tim wanted to run into. They looked at him with an expression . . . well, it was the expression of someone looking at the young man who'd killed their daughter. Suddenly the father held out his hand to Tim. "Thank you for coming," the father said.

"I'm so sorry . . ." Tim mumbled.

The mother went up to Tim and hugged him, saying she forgave him.

Those parents showed what forgiveness really is. It's not a feeling. It's hard to imagine that Tim would ever be anything other than a disturbing presence in their lives. He could never not be the boy who killed their daughter.

And yet their forgiveness was as real and genuine as possible. But it came from another place.

It was a decision. They hated what had happened and they quite possibly hated Tim for his part in it. But they decided that they wouldn't let what Tim had done stand between them and Tim.

That's what forgiveness is: a decision that you won't let what the other person did stand between the two of you any-more. You may have feelings of rage or resentment from time to time. But nonetheless, you will do your best to move forward with the relationship.

You might say, how can I decide that? I don't feel like forgiving. All right then, don't forgive. You can forgive when you're ready. It's okay if you're not ready yet.

It's just that I don't want you to wait around for some feeling of forgiveness to flow like warm honey through your veins, because that rarely happens. We'd all be in big trouble, if we had to depend on that happening. What you're not ready for yet is a decision to put your feelings of un-forgiveness behind you.

GETTING TO FORGIVENESS

How do you get to the point where you can make a decision to forgive the other person? Well, without your realizing it you've already completed a large part of the journey. At the beginning you were so disoriented and had so many questions that you almost thought you were going out of your mind.

But then gradually you got a sense that this betrayal was *not* going to destroy you.

You discovered through a painful process that the other person did care.

You learned that the other person could come to appreciate and understand how you really felt.

You came to believe that just possibly your relationship would survive.

And you found that the two of you could work together to make things safer and better in your relationship.

THE MISSING PIECE

There's really only one piece missing: reclaiming what was good in the relationship. Why is that important? It's important because relationships survive based on the good stuff in them, not the absence of bad stuff. Think about it. When you trust the other person, what are you trusting? That they won't hurt you, of course. But not being hurt by someone is not a reason to be in a relationship with them. You're in a relationship with someone because of the good things, not because of the bad things.

If the good things aren't there, why bother with the relationship, even if there aren't any bad things?

So far you've been working to get rid of the bad stuff. That's important because, as you well know, the bad stuff can easily pollute and poison the good stuff to the point where it seems gone. And if it is gone, there's no relationship. And if there's no relationship, well, forgiveness is still worthwhile, but really, between you and me, what difference does it make? If my husband's betrayal so many years ago plus the way I dealt with it had destroyed our relationship, forgiveness might be some comfort, but not much.

And the reason for that is that the possibility for forgiveness is woven into our DNA (or given to us by God, take your pick) because of its ability to promote reconciliation. Think of it this way: Imagine you were building a bookcase and you have all these pieces of wood. The wood is your relationship and forgiveness is the glue that holds it together. As you are repairing your damaged relationship, you're going through the wood and getting rid of the bad pieces—the rotted wood, the uneven cuts, the splintered pieces. But in order to build your bookcase, you need the good pieces—perfectly measured, cut and sanded, ready to be glued together.

Forgiveness glues relationships back together. Everything else sets up the possibility of reconciliation. Forgiveness creates the reconciliation.

And you can't get to forgiveness until and unless you reclaim the good stuff in your relationship.

Do the Six Questions Ever Blur Together?

I have to say something about the process of restoring trust and these six questions. It sounds so neat and orderly. You ask a question, get an answer, and move on to the next. But let's get real. Yes, the questions are real and they're pretty distinct, but sometimes they blur, and sometimes they even go out of order.

This is especially true for retrieving what's good in the relationship.

Let's take sex, for instance. Suppose sex was one of those things that was good in the relationship. Normally, you'd expect that the craziness and the anger and problem talk would pretty much eliminate sex until you got to this point. And sure enough that's often true.

But it's not necessarily true. I've seen situations, for example, where a woman has just found out that her guy has cheated on her and she's not just angry, she's crazy angry, and yet she'll suddenly insist on their having sex, maybe that very first night after the discovery of the affair. And she's the one initiating it. She can't believe she's doing this, and he certainly can't believe it, but it's happening anyway.

I've found that people will do things to reconnect to what was good in their relationship at every point in the trust-restoring process, even at the very beginning. For example, there's a married couple and one has terribly hurt the other. But they have kids and they realize that maintaining a good co-parenting relationship is more important than indulging in recriminations.

So they play with their kids and immediately experience something that's been very good in their relationship.

This is healthy. It's a way of laying the groundwork for the healing that's still to come.

Sure, the good things may be hard to access while you're still not trusting each other. But the fact that you can retrieve some good things gives you hope that trust building makes sense.

And when the two of you try to reconnect to what's been good, without realizing it you'll find that it takes you a long way toward rebuilding trust. You'll have renewed that feeling that it makes sense to be in this relationship, and if it makes sense to be in this relationship, you're less likely to do something to undermine it.

Sounds good, right? And it is good. But there's a huge pitfall here you have to be aware of. Maggie and Dave illustrate this point very well.

Maggie and Dave

Back when they were just going together, before they got engaged, Maggie discovered that Dave was an alcoholic. She briefly broke up with him but he begged her to take him back. She agreed because Dave was the sweetest, kindest, most loving guy she'd ever known.

She had one firm rule. She would only take him back if he promised to go to AA meetings at least once a week for the rest of their lives. She knew better than to get him to promise never to drink again. After all, people fall off the wagon. But going to meetings was something he had total control over. And if he loved her, he'd do it.

So Dave stopped drinking and went to meetings, they got engaged, and they got married. Not long after, Maggie noticed that things were going off-kilter. Mostly little things. One week Dave seemed to be behind in his work. Another week he lost some money. Then he got into a minor fender bender for which he seemed to have no good explanation.

One evening Dave left to go to his Monday night AA meeting, the one he most frequently attended. On an impulse Maggie followed him. Dave drove right past St. Margaret's, where they held the meetings in the basement, and drove on to the bowling alley where, Maggie knew, the drinks flowed freely. Maggie drove home and cried until Dave got back.

It felt like a terrible betrayal, not because of his drinking but because he no longer went to meetings. Maggie was more upset than she'd ever been in her life. It was as if a terrible abyss had opened up at her feet. She could accept that Dave wasn't perfect, but now clearly he was showing he didn't care enough to even try.

Maggie and Dave worked through almost all the questions. It was awful. It's always awful. But Dave seemed to be truly sorry, truly committed to never doing that again. And Maggie felt herself passing through that brief but all-important point where she felt it might be worthwhile hanging in there.

Working out their problems was an ordeal. It consisted mostly of her checking up on him to make sure that he was going to meetings. Sometimes he'd blow up at her for constantly being on his case, and she'd blow up at him for having been such a liar. But soon they settled into a rhythm. Dave was sober. There was every evidence that he was going to meetings. So Maggie began to feel that things *might be* okay with Dave and that they could enjoy being with each other again.

Might be. Possibly. But sometimes it turns out that "might be" is not enough to feel safe. Maggie tried to open up and let good things happen between them but she found that in spite of herself all she could do was create distance.

It was very unpredictable. One night they'd go out to a restaurant and have a good time. The next night Maggie wouldn't want to make herself available to Dave.

What was really going on?

YOUR GOOD STUFF VERSUS MY GOOD STUFF. Maggie and Dave were falling into the same dynamic lots of couples fall into. It comes about because the two people have radically different views of what "more of the good stuff" means.

Dave was thinking, everything is okay now because we're laughing and making love and having a nice meal together. Problem solved! The betrayal is behind us now. I'm not the bad guy anymore.

But that was the very *last* thing Maggie wanted him to be thinking. Her ability to trust him—to begin to trust him, really—depended on Maggie's continuing to see that Dave was aware that what he had done was a big deal and that she was still very vulnerable. Maggie was concerned not about their reconnecting to the good things, but that their reconnecting to the good things made Dave feel that everything is okay.

How did she remind him that everything was still not okay? Maggie withdrew from some of the good things they could do together. This darkness, distance, or withdrawal was her way of reminding him to stick with the program,.

But the pitfall goes further. Before you know it, a whole dynamic had developed. The more Dave tried to focus on making good things happen, the more Maggie felt she needed to remind him that everything wasn't yet all sweetness and light, that in fact the wound was completely unhealed. But the more Maggie went to this dark and distant place, the more Dave pushed her to cheer up, relax, and have fun. The next thing they knew, Dave was playing this card: "What's wrong with you for not being able to let go of this and move on? Maybe you need help. Maybe you should see someone."

And whenever the betrayer makes this move, the person in Maggie's situation sees red, which just made her seem as if she needed help all the more.

EVERYONE IS RIGHT. So what was the mistake here? What could they have done differently?

The mistake was thinking that it had to be either/or. Either we say, "Hey, let the good times roll." Or we focus on all the pain and mistrust still lying just under the surface.

The solution is to understand that both points of view can fully coexist. If you can enjoy being together, you should enjoy being together. If enjoying being together makes you suddenly feel vulnerable because you start thinking, "We're forgetting too soon," that's okay, too.

What you really need to do is say to each other something like this, "Look, we're in relationship rehab. We'll have good days and bad days. There will be times when we forget what's happened, and that's good. There will be times when we won't want to forget what's happened and that's okay, too." It's just like when a person is in rehab after a bad accident. You have good days and bad days. Days when you're making progress and days when it feels like you can't make progress. It's all part of making progress. You just have to let it all happen.

Healing a major betrayal is perfectly natural and, if you don't screw it up, inevitable. It's just that natural things don't go in a straight line. There are ups and downs. Roll with it.

PREVENTION

For people who are going through this, feeling their way to forgiveness, the question that keeps coming up is, *When do I start feeling safe?* There are three different, good answers to this question, and they're all true.

One answer is, never. I mean, come on: Would you trust me if I didn't acknowledge this possibility? If someone has hurt you, then it's a possibility that your unsafe feeling will never go away. Hopefully, because of the work you've done together, it's a much, much smaller possibility than it was before.

TWENTY-FIVE YEARS AGO, my husband, who was then a very young man, had a heart attack. I couldn't have imagined that happening. But it did. In the days and weeks and months that followed, I kept waiting for him to have another heart attack and, maybe, drop dead. But he went on to address the underlying problems that led to that heart attack. His blood pressure, cholesterol, and ability to deal with stress are all great now. He keeps going for tests and they keep showing up fine. He's in the risk category now of a healthy man of his age.

Have I forgotten about the possibility of his having a heart attack? No. That's still there in the back of my mind and somewhere in my heart. Because it happened once, it got put on the table and it can never be completely taken off the table.

At the same time, so what? I don't feel perfectly safe, but it doesn't hurt me or hurt us that I don't feel perfectly safe. Of course something bad could happen at any minute. But then, all kinds of bad things can happen at any minute. I just don't need to let these endless whispers of uncertainty pollute my day.

So when it comes to your own experience of being betrayed, yes, you might never be free of the fear that it could happen again, but you can easily be free from being crippled by that fear.

Reconnecting to the good things doesn't make the fear go away, but it does deprive that fear of its power. It soon becomes like background noise you don't pay attention to.

Now's the Time

Here's another good answer to the question When do I start feeling safe? Now. In fact, it's already happened. The fact that you can have moments or even long periods where you enjoy being with each other means that you're starting to feel safe now. Sure, you might get scared and wonder if feeling good means letting down your guard which means you're not safe. But then do this, which is far better than crapping all over the good things that are starting to creep back into your relationship. Just ask yourself, What do I need to feel reassured right now? It might be as simple as needing to ask the other person,

"Can you reassure me that you won't ever hurt me again the way you did before?" Hearing the answer to this question can be enormously helpful.

Here's the last good answer to the question When do I start feeling safe? Soon. And the reason the answer is soon is that there's something that's still needing to happen which usually takes place next: forgiveness.

FINALLY, FORGIVENESS

Imagine a world—and what a nice one it would be!—in which a pregnant woman would go into labor as she does now, with the contractions getting more and more intense, but then when it came time for the actual delivery the baby painlessly popped out like toast from a toaster. Sadly, we don't live in that world, but when it comes to forgiveness that is actually sort of how it goes most of the time.

The forgiveness that seemed impossible *just happens*. And of course it just happens because the groundwork has been laid. The anger has come out. You've learned that the other person really cares. You've discovered good things in each other again. You've solved the problems that led to the betrayal, many of them anyway. And so, amazingly, it becomes quite easy to decide to forgive.

It's especially easy, of course, when you understand that you don't have to wait for all feelings of anger and resentment to go away. You just have to decide that you will no longer let those feelings stand between you. And it will be even easier to make that decision because those feelings will have gotten a lot smaller.

There are other things going on that make it easy at this point to decide to forgive.

Sometimes we just get tired of not forgiving. The distance between you is demoralizing. The fear is exhausting. The resentment is draining. There rises up from deep within us a spiritual need to say, "Whatever."

Sometimes we become aware of how destructive it's been not to forgive. A good relationship has been getting chopped into little pieces. People close to you—children, friends, or colleagues—have gotten hurt. You yourself have become distracted and embittered. And you realize it's just not worth it to refuse to forgive.

Sometimes better understanding saves us. Through the process of problem-solving, seeing that you both had a part in what happened, you can realize that the other person did what he did not because he was a monster but because of a very human-sized problem that the both of you shared in.

This in fact is what happened with Ryan and Dawn. It took her a while, but Dawn eventually had a blinding and disturbing but ultimately healing insight: She realized that she herself might have had an affair if she'd been feeling the way Ryan had felt. So how could she not forgive him for doing what she herself might have done if she'd been in his shoes?

Sometimes the good things that have crept back into the relationship make it seem silly not to forgive. If you're laughing together, enjoying each other's company, perhaps making love, well then, haven't you already forgiven the other person? In this case, it's less of a decision than an acknowledgment of something that already exists.

And sometimes you just don't care anymore. I don't mean

that in a bad way. I just mean that you've suffered and struggled and worked through things, but you've also moved on. Time has passed. The betrayal feels more like something from history than a living reality. It's something that happened to a former self, something that was caused by the former self of the other person.

A BLESSED FORGETTING

There's a point you can reach that goes beyond forgiving. I hinted at it just now when I talked about how sometimes people move on from the betrayal. What I'm really talking about here is a kind of forgetting.

When there's been a betrayal people sometimes say, "Well, maybe I can forgive but I'll never forget." We too easily accept this as the best we can do. But it's not. Sure, when you're in the early stages it seems utterly impossible to forget. And on some level, of course, we don't ever forget. If you ask someone twenty-five years later, "Did your brother-in-law refuse to lend you $25,000 to help with the down payment on a house?" of course they will say yes.

But the kind of forgetting I'm talking about is where the hurt no longer lives in the front of your mind. It's like a picture that you take down from the wall and put in the bottom of a drawer. The picture still exists, but you no longer see it and it no longer comes into your thoughts.

This kind of forgetting is absolutely necessary. About ten years ago at a conference on reconciliation and forgiveness sponsored by the Templeton Foundation, Archbishop Desmond Tutu said "The remembrance of past grievances was the single most significant obstacle to reconciliation and forgiveness."

Why is that? Imagine you're running your hand over a rough piece of lumber. You know that if there's any little splinter sticking out it will pierce your skin. Well, not being able to forget leaves us vulnerable to grievance the way splinters leave us vulnerable to being pierced. If we don't forget, we keep getting snagged by one grievance after another.

Forgetting is a kind of smoothing out of the rough wood of memory. The hurts are sanded away. There's nothing on which to get snagged.

I can see this in my own life. I know I've told you about how my husband betrayed me many years ago. But honestly, the whole experience is like looking at an old high school yearbook. The memories come back, but they seem like memories from a different time. They seem like the memories of a former self.

You remember the fact of the pain, but you don't feel the pain. The grievances are gone.

And how exactly do you accomplish this miracle? Again, it's easier and happens more naturally than you might think. Again, we're designed by nature to let go of grievances that are no longer relevant and to lose our memory of them.

TWO MEMORY ERASERS. Two things work to erase the memory of the betrayals you've experienced. And we've talked about both of them.

The first memory eraser is the good things that happen between you and the other person. Every pleasant phone call, every cheery email or text, every fun get-together for lunch, every experience of affection, every gesture of real support, every shared accomplishment—all these, any of these, put a vast, memory-erasing distance between you and the bad thing that happened.

It's hard to believe this at first because, frankly, it's not our first experience. Early on in the trust-restoring process we have an almost opposite experience. We're still haunted by the betrayal and then something good somehow manages to happen between us and the other person. And yet next thing we know, the memory of the betrayal comes roaring back. It almost feels as if a brief moment of forgetting is a prelude to remembering again even more strongly.

But that changes dramatically over time. As the weeks and months go by, those positive experiences work to extinguish bad memories instead of stimulating them. It's like when you've been sick and you get out of bed for the first time. Initially standing up makes you feel worse. But the more you stand up and move around, the better you feel eventually. The movements that made you remember your pain end up helping you forget your pain.

The second memory eraser is all the things the person who betrayed you does to specifically make up for his betrayal. If he betrayed by being disloyal, he helps to erase that memory every time he does something loyal, beyond the call of duty. If he betrayed by abandoning you, he helps erase that memory every time he's there for you. If he hurt you, he erases that memory every time he does something kind or sweet or generous.

He doesn't have to go to heroic lengths. I'm not talking about one of those "I'll spend the rest of my life making this up to you" situations. In fact, the notion of "going to heroic lengths" can actually perpetuate a cycle of grievance. No, I'm just talking about the good, decent, helpful things that people can and should do in their relationships all the time. And my point is that these acts of normal goodness, to the extent that they go in the opposite direction from the betrayal, lead to a blessed forgetting.

LOOKING AHEAD

So that's how you restore trust after a major betrayal. I've shown you what to do that will work. I've shown you how it's all based on your getting answers to six key questions. I've shown you the pitfalls to avoid.

This information is tremendously useful for dealing with any of the ways mistrust enters a relationship, not just a major betrayal. There are other situations that can be just as destructive as a major betrayal in their own ways, and each has special features that need to be addressed separately. And that's what we're going to do next.

Part Three

RESTORING
TRUST IN OTHER
SITUATIONS

12

When the Other Person Is Unreliable

WHEN YOU USE the word *betrayal* in the context of relationships, the first thing everyone thinks about is someone having an affair. The next thing they think about is some other major betrayal. What all these have in common is that there's been one huge hard-to-swallow event that knocks everyone sideways, like a car crash.

But focusing on a major betrayal is too limited. What is a betrayal anyway? It's when you have an expectation of someone—a normal, reasonable expectation—and the other person violates it. You might think it's unreasonable to use a big-impact word like *betrayal* for a small disappointment. So, okay: If it's a small disappointment, it's a small betrayal. Fine. It's still the case that whenever an expectation is violated, it feels like a betrayal.

If your airline cancels your flight while you're standing at the gate, you're going to feel betrayed. You expect, and had a right to expect, that when you bought your ticket the airline would carry out the promise it made to have a plane take you where you wanted to go at the agreed-upon time. They said they were going to do that. You took that as a promise. You relied on that promise. And so if it doesn't happen, you're going to have all the bad feelings we associate with betrayal.

Betrayal is a kind of reliability breakdown. Then let me ask you this: Which is worse, one big betrayal or a seemingly endless series of little betrayals? If you were about to say one big betrayal and then hesitated, good for you. Of course anything can happen with any two people. But in general, relationships have an easier time dealing with one big betrayal than an endless series of little ones.

It kind of makes sense when you think about it. If someone hurts you in some big way and is then sorry and promises never to do it again, part of you wants to believe that promise. And there's a good chance you'll be right to believe it. People can do awful things and then never do them again.

Repeated little betrayals can be much harder to deal with. They feel like they are a more coordinated attack on your ability to trust.

Here's an example.

Matthew and Stephanie

When my kids were in school, one of them came home one day with a great saying: *When you assume you make an ASS out of U and ME*. Truer words were never spoken, words that Stephanie should have heeded. What she assumed was that since Matthew was a good guy and a good catch (He was rich! He was hand-some!), he'd be the kind of husband she wanted. And since she was a go-getter, she wanted a husband who was a go-getter, too.

Well Matthew wasn't like that at all. He was like Ferdinand the Bull in the children's book. All Matthew really wanted to do, so to speak, was lie under a tree and smell the flowers. To putter with his hobbies. To live a quiet life.

That sure wasn't the way Stephanie wanted to live. Her image of the way things were supposed to be was two people hopping from cocktail party to cocktail party while the husband, in whatever free time he had, was building treehouses for the kids and coaching their soccer team.

Matthew could have stopped this train wreck of clashing needs anytime he wanted. He could have just said no to Steph-anie's incessant demands. But she was unrelenting and got so angry when he said no, and besides she was so pretty, that his strategy became I'll say yes to everything but I won't do it.

MEET MR. UNRELIABLE. I don't know on what planet Mat-thew thought this solution would actually work, but certainly not on Planet Stephanie. Every time he agreed to do something, he was basically making a contract with her. From Stephanie's point of view, her life with him was an endless series of broken contracts, broken promises. And it made her crazy. She was mar-ried to Mr. Unreliable.

And that's the thing about this problem. When you're in a relationship with Mr. or Ms. Unreliable, your life can easily take on a nightmarish quality. You can't count on anything. It feels as if trust is impossible. With a major betrayal, there's at least a part of you—if only a tiny part of you—that believes the other person's promise that he'll never do it again. But when there's endless little betrayals, trust has proven to be foolish.

There are lots of ways this can happen besides someone never doing what they say they are going to do.

There's the situation where the other person lies all the time.

There's the situation where the other person is always getting into trouble.

There's the situation where the other person is emotionally volatile or unstable.

There's the situation where the other person keeps failing at her job.

There's even the situation where the other person keeps getting sick. It might not seem fair to label that betrayal because it isn't deliberate, but that's often the way it feels, whether we like it or not.

STUBBORN HOPE. At this point, you might be asking a great question: Why do people stay in a relationship like this? If you can't count on the other person, just leave.

Of course, many people do leave in these kinds of situations. But it's harder than you might think.

Hope is a stubborn thing. For some reason, we are likely to hang in there as long as we have hope that the other person will stop being the way he is. Stephanie had this hope because Matthew kept promising he would do things. Even when we have a hard time believing these kinds of promises anymore, we can't completely disbelieve them either. There's something about someone looking you in the eye and making a promise that makes you *want to believe.*

RARE WINS ARE ADDICTIVE. Another reason people hang in there grows out of the well-established psychological law of intermittent reinforcement.

To see this law in action, look no farther than your nearest casino. Everyone who gambles loses far more often than they win. But every once in a while, even the unluckiest person will win at slots or blackjack. And something weird happens to us when we get a rare reward like this. It's intoxicating. In fact (and countless experiments have demonstrated this), being rewarded occasionally keeps people hanging in there far more diligently than they would otherwise.

And when someone who's usually unreliable comes through, as even the most unreliable person does every once in a while, that person's partner takes this as a reward and is more likely to hang in there. When I explained this law to Stephanie she said, "Oh my God, so that's how the bastard does it. Every once in a while Matthew will keep one of his stupid promises."

Of course, if you think about this for a moment, you can see how dangerous this is. The law of intermittent reinforcement turns people into compulsive gamblers who throw away their life savings. It keeps people hanging on, earning $5,000 or $10,000 a year as bit actors in Hollywood hoping for that big break. And when it comes to relationships, it keeps people involved with partners who can't be counted on.

BLINDED TO THE DANGERS. Let me be real specific about what the danger is. It's that the occasional reward blinds you to your net return. This is why a guy will stay with a woman who's generally mean to him (when she's not ignoring him) just because every once in a while she's really nice to him. (By the way, that supposed phenomenon of why men like bitches is exactly this.) And this is why women will stay with men who rarely treat them right except for being sweet every once in a while.

When I ask these people, "Do the good things make up for the bad times?" most people in these situations say no and yet it's hard for them to leave.

I can imagine you hearing this with your heart in your mouth. What am I actually suggesting? Is your relationship doomed?

I'm not suggesting you leave just because you're involved with someone who's unreliable. I am strongly suggesting that you not deceive yourself. There are plenty of areas in life where the good things more than make up for the bad, even if the good things are relatively rare. For example, the paycheck you get at the end of every month might more than make up for the hours of labor you put in every day. And so that's fine, as long as you're not deceiving yourself.

So how do you not deceive yourself when you're involved with someone who's unreliable—that is, someone who fills your life with small and not-so-small disappointments?

The answer is you keep an account. Here's how. Every day in your journal or your calendar you write down either a Y or an N. Y means "Yes, I would stay in this relationship if every day for the rest of my life were like today." N means, "No, I would not stay in this relationship if I knew that every day for the rest of my life would be like today."

Then at the end of a month you add up the Ys and the Ns. If the Ns outnumber the Ys, then you have to ask yourself if you're deceiving yourself by staying in this relationship. Remember, if there are more Ns than Ys, then if you stay in this relationship, you're choosing to stay in a relationship where the bad times outweigh the good times. If that's worth it to you, fine. But the question is, Are you really sure it's worth it to you?

How Do You Trust Someone Who Is Reliably Unreliable?

Suppose you've decided to stay. Fine. But you still have to heal the broken trust. After all, you just can't be happy staying with someone if your days are eaten up with mistrust. Because even if staying feels worthwhile now, the accumulation of mistrust and disappointment can easily corrode your good feelings. I see people who come to me all the time who, after five, ten, twenty years of dealing with an unreliable person say "I just couldn't take it anymore."

How do you let go and forgive when the other person is continuing to disappoint you?

First of all, *is* the other person being consistently unreliable? Is she really always showing up late the way she used to? Is she continuing to tell little fibs the way she used to? Is she as forgetful as she used to be?

Think before you answer. It's easy to be mistaken here. You see, most of us put halos—both positive and negative—around the people in our lives.

HALOS. Here's how it works. When someone has a positive halo, we tend to notice the good things about them and ignore the bad. When someone has a negative halo, we tend to notice the bad things about them and ignore the good. This phenomenon is why, for example, there's so often tension between young adults and their parents. The parents remember the way these young adults were as teens, and so of course there's a huge negative halo. But the young adults are usually now much more responsible; it's just that their parents can't see it because of the negative halo. And it is, as you can imagine, extremely annoying to be treated as irresponsible when in fact you're pretty together now.

So look at the other person in your life with fresh eyes. Isn't it possible that he has actually gotten better?

IN A NEW LIGHT. Another way you might find your way back to trust is if you look at the other person in a new light. Yes, this person is unreliable, but perhaps you can think of him as *reliably* unreliable.

What does that mean? It means you can trust how unreliable they are.

That can make a huge difference. None of us is perfect. But we're not randomly imperfect. My imperfections have a certain predictability about them and I'm sure yours do, too.

If you're involved with someone who is reliably unreliable, at some point it becomes your fault if you don't allow for the way the other person is. If you and I are friends and you know that I'm usually late, you've got two choices. You can continually get upset about it, as if every time I was late it was a big news flash for you. Or you can say, Oh, that Mira, she's always late so I'm certainly not going to make a huge effort to be on time when I'm meeting her, and if she's offered to drive me to the airport I'll tell her to be at my house two hours before I really need her to be there or find another way to get there. Do you see how easy it can be?

Ellie's story

I once worked with a woman, Ellie, whose husband was always telling little fibs. He wasn't a bad person, but he'd picked up this bad habit from being brought up by very controlling parents. When he was a kid, the best way he could think of to protect himself from them was to hide the truth. It worked well enough then for it to become a habit, and it stuck.

After years of seething and occasionally blowing up at her husband's fibs, Ellie had a startling realization: The very predictability of these fibs, which had been her torment, could be her salvation. All she had to do was stop being surprised by what in fact was inevitable. Because let's face it, if it's inevitable, it ain't a surprise.

Once Ellie started expecting her husband's fibs, she was able to roll with it. Instead of responding harshly—which had just made her seem controlling like his parents and therefore made him want to fib even more—she relaxed; got happy and friendly; and said in a mild, non-threatening voice, "Oh Hal, I know you're fibbing, which is fine, but I'd really appreciate it if now you told the truth."

And more often than not he would. Her decision to trust him made him trust her. And there you have it: yet one more example of how trust breeds trust and makes things better.

NO MISTAKES, NO PROBLEM

So what are the mistakes people make when it comes to trying to restore trust with someone who is unreliable?

One is that they fail to honestly assess how toxic the situation is. Because if it really is bad, you'd better know it. And we've talked about that.

Second, if this really is a bad situation for you, you need to end the relationship. Don't make the mistake of staying in a relationship that isn't working for you. And we've talked about that.

Third, open your eyes to the possibility that the other person has changed. Sometimes people do change and we just don't see it. And we've talked about that.

Fourth, don't make the mistake of thinking that you can't work with what you've got. If the other person is reliably unreliable, then you may well be able to live with it by factoring it into your calculations. And we've talked about that.

So how, finally, do you let go and find trust and forgiveness with someone who is unreliable?

To do this, you need to understand the part both of you play in this drama. Here's how it works with most of the people I've seen.

John and Jane

Let's call the couple John and Jane and let's say that John is unreliable in lots of ways. He forgets things, he's late, he fibs, he screws up. Is this guy a walking disaster? Or is he a good guy whose standards are, shall we say, a little looser than Jane's? Who knows. The fact is that by the time they come to me for help Jane is furious and John is furious with Jane for being furious with him. That's the pattern. That's always the pattern.

But, ah!, it didn't start out that way. Maybe Jane didn't no-

tice John's unreliability at first or maybe she noticed it but tried
to ignore it. In any case, according to the most common pattern,
Jane would try to smother her discontent until it exploded out
of her. That's the way a lot of us women are. We only become
the psycho-bitch from hell after we've struggled to be the Queen
of Nice for as long as we could stand it. But by the time we reach
the snapping point, our nerves are worn raw.

At this point, every little screw-up sends us around the bend.
So when John forgot to pick up their daughter from pre-school,
Jane blew up. But Jane also blew up with equal force when John
forgot to bring home a bottle of milk.

HOW THE DYNAMIC PLAYS OUT. Stay with me and watch the
dynamic John and Jane get into. He keeps screwing up. Her
nerves eventually get worn raw. Now she gets royally pissed at
every screw-up. And now he feels he's entered a world where the
relative importance of things has gotten lost completely.

Think about it. Here you have a loosey-goosey guy to begin
with and now he's getting the message that it doesn't matter
what he does—big mistakes, little mistakes, they're all responded
to in the same way. And then people in his situation always respond in the same way: "If she blows up at me when I make a
small mistake even though I've just done my best to get some
big thing right, then why bother? If I'm going to get into trouble
no matter what, then why make any effort?"

So you see how this works. In the ways they respond to each
other, John and Jane and almost any couple in their situation
take a path that leads from bad to worse. The more John screws
up, the more Jane's nerves get worn raw and the more likely she
is to explode at every screw-up. The more often she explodes at

big and little screw ups, the more likely he is to think that what he does doesn't matter. Her hyper-vigilance and hyper-reactivity, which feel to her like they should motivate him to become reliable, actually have the effect of promoting his unreliability.

It would be nice to say that the whole problem could be solved if John were just more reliable. Well, does it work to ask someone to be more reliable?

Actually, it does, if you do it right. You see, most unreliable people are that way because they're in rebellion against being controlled. Trying to control their unreliability actually feeds their unreliability. So that's a mistake. Don't do that.

HERE'S WHAT WORKS. You say, "It would mean a lot to me, it would make me really happy, if you [. . . and just fill in here whatever is important to you, like "bring home milk when I ask you to and you've agreed to it"]. Is there anything I can do to help you with that?"

This is a complete game-changer. You have now taken yourself out of the control business, and so he doesn't have to be in the resisting-control business. I promise you: This works beautifully.

With two qualifications. And I know because I've done this with my husband, to say nothing of all the couples I've worked with.

The first qualification is that no one is going to turn on a dime. And that's hard for us when our nerves are worn raw. Maybe it's too late: If your patience is shot beyond hope of redemption, then your relationship is probably shot, too. A troubled relationship can't survive the loss of patience.

But if you can be patient, you will see a miracle unfold in

front of your eyes. As you stop being so controlling, and as he comes to believe that you're really not so controlling, and as you focus on telling him what you need to be happy, he will come around. Slowly at first, but then more quickly.

Which leads to the second qualification. Unreliable people seldom become perfectly reliable. People who forget become much better at remembering but they'll still occasionally forget. Fibbers will still fib, although much less often.

So you have to look into your heart. If you need perfection, then you shouldn't be with someone who is unreliable. It will just drive the two of you nuts. But if you'll be happy with things getting better, maybe a little, maybe a lot, then they really *can* get better.

So that's how it works here for getting to the point of restoring trust and forgiveness when unreliability is the issue. The other person has made the huge mistake of being unreliable. But for sure you, too, have made a mistake in how you deal with it.

On the principle that everyone should correct their own mistakes, you have a lot more power to make things better than you might have thought. It's not your fault that this whole thing started in the first place. But if you accept that you have a part in making things better, then they can and will get better. And the trust will start to flow back and forth between you again.

MAKING PROGRESS. And what about Matthew and Stephanie? What happened with them?

There's no one I respect more than people who make progress slowly. It's easy to give up. It's easy to stay motivated when there's quick progress. But to hang in there when progress is slow, that's an achievement in itself.

And that's where Matthew and Stephanie are. What's keeping them on the slow path, as both of them have acknowledged, is . . . well, let Stephanie explain in her own words:

"With us, it's two steps forward, one step back. I'm patient and Matthew makes progress, but he's not perfect and sometimes he screws up and sometimes I lose it, which sets us back. It's been very hard for me to realize that I'm as bad at making things better as Matthew is at being reliable. But that's good, too, because it's easier for me to accept his not being perfect when I accept my not being perfect. And then I'm less likely to blow up, which makes him less likely to screw up. We're not there yet, but we're definitely getting there."

13

Power Issues

U P UNTIL NOW, we've been looking at situations where mistrust comes because of the way a person behaves. He screws
up; you lose trust. But that's just one of the ways mistrust happens between two people. Mistrust can appear because of who
someone is or because of ways two people are different. Power
differences are among the most important causes of mistrust.

Many of us aren't used to thinking in terms of ourselves or
other people in our life having power. Sure, your boss has "boss
power." There's a lot more of your doing what he wants than of
his doing what you want. That's power! You can see how powerful a sick toddler might be. Or a frantic bride-to-be. A woman
going into labor will probably be pretty powerful because everyone will be rushing around to meet her needs.

Let's look at how this comes up in relationships.

Annie and Doug

For many years, Doug earned a lot more money than Annie did. They had thought that this didn't create much of a power imbalance since their agreement was that they would discuss all major purchases, which they did (though, Annie later realized, her voice had too often been squelched).

But then things got turned around. Annie got a big promotion and Doug quit his job to start a small business with a close friend. Suddenly he had no money and she had all the money. To the surprise of both of them, this made a huge difference. She'd thought that things had been balanced. But now that she made all the money, she realized how much she'd squelched her own voice. It went very deep. She started remembering all the times she'd put her own needs on the back burner, such as her wanting another child, or her wanting them to sell the summer house they had, which she really disliked.

The net result of this shift in their lives was that a tidal wave of mistrust washed over their relationship. Doug had trouble trusting her because, from his point of view, she suddenly started lording it over him now that she was the one who paid the piper. But Annie had trouble trusting Doug. Feeling disempowered, he started throwing his weight around in a way he'd not done when he'd earned most of the money. Now, instead of just going ahead and making a decision on his own, or just out-arguing her if there was a discussion, he'd get upset until he got his way. Each now saw the other as unreasonable, demanding, and power hungry.

But all the change in their relative earning power did was highlight a dynamic that had been there all along. Power imbalances are always a risk factor for mistrust. Doug and Annie just hadn't seen it because their earlier arrangement had seemed normal to them: it just seemed "normal" for the guy to make more money and have final say in their key decisions. When their lives changed, the power dynamic changed, too—she had the money now and, as the saying goes, she who pays the piper calls the tune—and their trust issues came out.

How could it not be like this? Think about it. To the extent that you have power over me, you can do things that affect me and I can't do anything about it. That's what power means. So how can I trust you if to some extent you can do what you want to me?

Of course, most people don't have power because they're power mad, and they don't lose power because they're weak. Power differences usually just come from the circumstances of people's lives. But differences in power have huge implications for people's ability to trust. For many relationships, all you have to do is list the power imbalances—for example, she gets very emotional, which he can't cope with, while he has a job in which many people depend on him so she doesn't feel she can question any work-related decision—and you have an instant map to all the trust issues between the two. And you can't heal the mistrust unless you understand where the trust issues come from.

Brian and Lisa

First comes love, then comes marriage. It's such an old story and for Brian and Lisa it started so innocently. How could anything go wrong? And yet things went very, very wrong indeed. When things were at their worst, there was deep mistrust all around.

Brian and Lisa met in college. It was one of those relation-ships where a young woman, tired of all the jerks she's been in-volved with, is attracted to a handsome, honest, considerate guy who seems very comfortable in himself. And the young guy, after all the game players he's gotten involved with, is attracted to a sweet, kooky, affectionate young woman. Yes, they were very different people, but each seemed to have just what the other was looking for.

At one point early on he asked her what her father did, and it turned out he was an old-fashioned country doctor. Nice! When she asked what his father did, Brian vaguely talked about his dad owning a business. Lisa imagined a small store.

Brian left out one detail. His father was, in fact, a very suc-cessful contractor. But Brian hadn't wanted to say anything for a couple of reasons. First, he was embarrassed in front of this simple country girl by the fact that his family had a lot of money, which he hadn't earned. But he also was cautious. He'd had so many experiences of how his family's business gave people the wrong idea—that he was somehow really rich, which he himself wasn't, not yet anyway. He needed to know that whomever he married was marrying him for the right reasons.

So it wasn't until they'd fallen in love and gotten engaged that Brian started letting Lisa know what she was getting in-volved with. Brian was charmed all over again by how thrilled Lisa was that she was marrying into a successful family business. She didn't even try to be cool about it. Somehow this reassured Brian. He was even more reassured when he met her father, who, true to his country-doctor credentials, didn't seem to give a damn about how much money someone had.

Lisa sobered up quite a bit when she saw the prenup she was expected to sign. It wasn't a complete surprise—she expected it, given that she was marrying into a family business—but the terms seemed . . . tightfisted. The terms weren't exactly punitive, but if they got divorced without any children, Lisa got close to nothing. Even if Brian died in the first few years of their marriage, Lisa wouldn't exactly become a rich woman. Whatever generosity there was in this agreement was all for whatever kids might come.

They got married soon after graduation, and Brian immediately went to work in the family business. And that's when Lisa began to see more and more clearly that, in this case anyway, money certainly did not mean freedom. Their lives were all about their responsibilities and duties. Trips he just had to take. Luncheons she just had to attend. People she just had to let work in their house.

It had never occurred to Lisa that getting married into a family business could be so disempowering for her, but it was. She was simply not free to make a lot of the kinds of decisions that a woman starting married life would normally be able to make: no, couldn't get rid of that hideous curio cabinet because his mother would freak out. She began to see why this nobody—as she referred to herself—was attractive to Brian. He must have instinctively felt that her innocence would prevent her from noticing her enslavement. It's not that she thought he duped her—he must have just taken his life for granted—but she had certainly not done her due diligence.

What with all the demands and expectations on her—including the occasional urgent need for her to fill in at the office—Lisa had no power at all, and she felt it.

THE ACCOUNTABILITY ISSUE. Brian had so much wanted to marry someone who loved him for himself, but now that they were married Lisa felt that Brian neither knew her nor cared about her, not as she actually was. Lisa had always been fascinated by Princess Di and now it felt like an eerie premonition. Lisa now understood perfectly well how Princess Di must have felt being embraced and discarded all at the same time. The message she got was: "We love you and want you, but you have to totally subsume yourself to the needs of the family business. You're perfect as long as you don't have a self that doesn't fit into our needs."

The last straw for Lisa was when she talked to Brian about wanting to go off with a friend for a couple of days. She knew she had demands to meet at home. But so what? It wasn't just that Brian put his foot down. It was what he said: "Get with the program." She'd never felt so helpless, even as a little girl. And you can't trust someone who makes you feel helpless.

One of the worst parts—and certainly the most destructive part—of any power imbalance is lack of trust. Just think about it. *Power is the ability to do what you want and get away with it.* The more power someone else has, the less you can do what you want. So the other person doesn't have to take you into account. He can, if he wants, consult only his own needs. And how can you totally trust someone like that?

Suppose you're driving far from home and your car breaks down and is towed to some small-town repair shop. The garage guy has all the power. He can say the problem is whatever he wants, and there's very little you can do about it. If he says the engine blew a gasket and it'll cost $2,500 to repair, what can you do besides blow a gasket yourself? So you see how someone else having power erodes your trust. And if you can't see it, it may be because you haven't been hurt by someone with power. How lucky you are in your innocence! But once a person has been hurt by someone with power, because of that power, then forever on power itself will be a sign of jeopardy. Just ask any person going into a second marriage whose first spouse misused his power. And this is what happened for Lisa. She was accountable to Brian. There were all kinds of family and business obligations. But he wasn't accountable to her. He was always coming home late or going off on trips or bringing people home, all without any notice.

THE BIRTH OF MISTRUST. So where exactly did the mistrust come in for Brian and Lisa? Well, since Brian could do whatever he wanted without any accountability, Lisa was never able to be sure about what he was doing and why he was doing it. He could say he was working late, but maybe he was just out drinking with some buddies. He could say he was going on a business trip, but it could just as easily be a golfing trip.

You might say that she should just trust him, that trust is the foundation of marriage, that it's all about trust, blah, blah, blah. And that's true. But when one person has a lot more power than another, the bonds of trust are loosened. And this reveals one of the deep truths about trust: *We trust because there's accountability.* Accountability can narrow a power differential. Lack of accountability heightens power differentials. For example, if you ask me to drive you to the airport and I say yes, I suddenly have power—you're going to want to keep me happy in case I don't show up—but this power is limited by the fact that I'm accountable to you. We're friends amidst a network of friends. If I stand you up, everyone will know.

You trust me because you know that I know that I'll have to face real consequences if I screw up.

Brian didn't face any real accountability. There were no consequences because there was no way for Lisa to know for sure what he was doing. The more power someone has, the fewer consequences he faces for his actions. And if you're dealing with someone who doesn't have to face any consequences for what he does, it's hard to trust him.

And here's another thing about mistrust. It grows, like mold. It festers and feeds on itself. We speculate, and those speculations plant seeds in our mind that lead to further mistrust.

And that's what happened to Lisa. Once she realized that Brian could be doing whatever he wanted, the possibility of his business trip being a golf outing turned into the possibility he was with another woman, which turned into the possibility that he had a long-time mistress, just like Prince Charles's Camilla Parker-Bowles.

DEALING WITH TRUST ISSUES ARISING FROM POWER DIFFERENCES

You might be wondering how this applies to you. After all, you're probably not in a relationship with the son of a successful contractor. (Or in a relationship with the heir to the British throne, for that matter!)

But here are some power differences that come up in everyday life and yet have a surprising ability to sow the seeds of mistrust.

- He is a social worker who helps desperate people in need, and so she feels her needs don't have much weight in the balance. He has power relative to her.

- She is really, *really* smart. He? Not so much. Her ability to out-think and out-argue him leaves him feeling helpless in any disagreement. She can always prove why she is right and he is wrong.

- He is a good son with a sick mother. Whenever his mother needs something, which is often, he jumps to do it. His mother's needs mean he can't say no to her, which makes it hard for him to say yes to his wife. He has less power relative to his mother, but more power relative to his wife.

- She gets very upset very easily, dramatically so. She freaks out so intensely that he doesn't feel he can stand up to her. Often, being very emotional is a way to re-empower yourself in the face of someone who has a lot of power. In this case, though, she is just a very emotional person, so all else being equal this would give her more power.

THE ENDLESS STRUGGLE FOR POWER. This last situation was Lisa's solution to dealing with Brian. It's not that she chose it deliberately. But power is like water: it always finds its own level. Whenever someone is disempowered they will find ways to re-empower themselves. So if you suddenly have power over me, how can you trust me not to want to find ways to resist, evade, and oppose your power? (Just think of what often happens on jobs when one person is made supervisor over someone who the day before had been her equal co-worker.) Every parent of toddlers or teenagers (been there, done that!) knows how kids gain power for themselves—like throwing a tantrum—to match any attempt of yours to assert power.

It's the basic paradox of power. The minute a power difference occurs, the disempowered person will do things to try to re-empower herself. This increase in her power will make the other person feel disempowered and then he'll try to re-empower himself. Because of this dynamic of power and resistance, *both* parties are likely to feel that the other is more powerful. Both feel relatively disempowered. *In at least three-quarters of couples, both people feel the other is more powerful.*

Lisa's feelings of disempowerment grew out of feelings of helplessness, which led to anger, frustration, and despair. Which eventually led to emotional outbursts. She didn't plan any of this. It just happened. She really did feel upset.

But that's when she made a big discovery. The more upset she got, the more likely Brian was to try to give her what she wanted! It was as if by getting upset she turned into a crying baby whom he would desperately try to pacify. And the more upset she got, the more power she had over Brian.

And what would you guess was Brian's response to this sudden, huge increase in Lisa's power? That's right: *He* found it hard to trust *her*. He sensed immediately that she could get whatever she wanted by getting upset. So why should he trust that she wouldn't misuse this power? It turned out that there was very little cost to her from exercising this power. It seemed as though she could get what she wanted without any consequences. Which is just like the power a man has walking into a bank with a sawed-off shotgun.

Pretty soon Brian and Lisa were in a power standoff. Each felt that the other could do whatever he or she wanted, while each felt that he himself (or she herself) could no longer get what they wanted.

Power struggles like that are always mutually disempowering. They generate fear and distance instead of solutions. And yet they're almost inevitable as long as one person feels relatively disempowered.

And of course both people end up in a state of mistrust and suspicion.

So how do you climb out of this hole?

DEALING WITH THE POWER IMBALANCE

We can't eliminate power imbalances in relationships. What we can do is deal with these power imbalances in a way that doesn't damage trust. And that's good enough for most people. Let me show you how to do that.

But you should be aware that this issue can't always be solved. It's not because of the size of the power imbalance. It's because one of the people is what I call a power person.†

Lots of us have power. Some of us even seek power. And

---

† I have a whole discussion about power people starting on page 66 of *Too Good to Leave, Too Bad to Stay*. This is the chapter in this book people ask me about more than any other.

there's nothing wrong with that. The world needs its movers and shakers.

But power people are different. A power person just wants to win, period. A normal person can have a lot of power and still be committed to fairness. But a power person isn't interested in fairness.

A normal woman, for example, might quite appropriately have a lot of power in her job but she has no need to dominate people in the workplace or at home. But if she's a power person, her attempts at gaining control just won't stop.

Rita and Larry

With an ordinary powerful person, you'll feel that you can get your needs met. Rita was married to Larry, a brilliant and articulate trial lawyer, who could easily out-argue her in any discussion. But here's how we know he wasn't a power person. One day in a couples therapy session she said to him, "Look, honey, you can out-argue me on any issue. I can never out-argue you. But that means that every time we discuss doing something you win. So I end up never getting any of my needs met. Is that fair?"

He looked at her for a moment and then took her hand. "No," he said, "that's not fair. It's not fair unless we're both getting our needs met in this relationship. But I don't know how to fix this."

That's when I chimed in. "I've got a perfect tool for you guys. I'll show you. Tell me about something you've recently argued about."

"Well," she said, "we were just talking about where to go out to eat after we leave here and I wanted to have Italian food but he talked me out of it. But I still want Italian food."

"Perfect," I said. "Here's what you do. Each of you assign a number to your preference." (Remember this from earlier in the book?) I turned to him and asked, "Where would you like to eat?"

"I've been thinking Japanese," he said.

"Fine," I said. "So tell me then: On a scale from 1 to 10, where 1 means you just don't care and 10 means you want it as much as you ever wanted anything, what number would you give for your preference for Japanese food tonight?"

"Well, I want Japanese, but I guess I'd say, I don't know, a 6."

"And what is it for you to have Italian food," I asked Rita.

"Well, I mean, it's not life-or-death, and I know it's fattening, but . . . honestly? It's a 9. I've been craving Italian food all week. Maybe it's stupid but that's how I feel. It's a 9."

Larry stared at Rita as if he'd had a revelation. "My God, Rita, if I'd known it mattered that much to you of course I would've said let's have Italian food."

And off they went to an Italian restaurant.

Larry was powerful, but he wasn't a power person. He cared about Rita and he cared about being fair. A power person would have found a way to short-circuit any fair process. And if by chance he couldn't get what he wanted he'd make such a stink that you'd regret having gotten what you wanted. But by avoiding discussions and going right to assigning a number to their preference, Larry and Rita kept arriving at choices that felt fair to both of them.

That's what to watch for when we talk about how to restore trust when there's a power imbalance. The other person might give you a hard time, but does he or she basically come down on the side of fairness? Or does he always have to win?

I'll tell you this: If the other is a power person, you'll never be happy being in a relationship with him. It's time to leave. A power person won't care about how much you have a craving for Italian food. He just wants to get what he wants. Your needs just don't matter. And power people never change.

GAIN UNDERSTANDING. When it comes to restoring trust in a relationship where there's a power imbalance, the first mistake people make is not talking to each other about what's really going on. They deal with their sense of helplessness by trying to gain power rather than trying to gain understanding. The solution that works is to begin by sitting down and talking to each other.

Here's the thing: People almost always seem more powerful than they feel. In fact, **the less powerful someone feels, the more likely she is to do things to gain power.** I think of this as almost a law of nature, the way apples fall down instead of up. So it follows that the more things she does to gain power, the less powerful she's actually feeling. A crying baby is a good example of this.

By talking, all this comes out.

Remember Brian and Lisa? Lisa was astounded to learn that Brian felt as disempowered by his role in the family business as she felt disempowered by her role. While it seemed to Lisa that Brian was calling all the shots, Brian felt that he wasn't in charge of anything. Those late nights and those business trips were forced on him as much as they were forced on her.

And he learned that Lisa's getting upset to the point where she was scary crazy were expressions of her own feelings of help-lessness.

The more they talked, the more they realized how utterly powerless they both had been feeling. And that was a huge step toward their being able to help each other.

So if you're feeling mistrust, resentment, and frustration, have a conversation about power.

Talk about how powerful you feel the other person is, and how little power you feel you have.

Don't try to correct the other person's impressions. That will just lead to a fight. If you're ever going to rebuild trust, you have to know how powerful you seem to the other person and how powerless he feels compared to you.

Overcoming the Three Obstacles to Trust

Okay, so you've started talking. Now, how do you rebuild trust?

When there's a power imbalance there are three obstacles to restoring trust.

1. You feel in the dark

2. You feel helpless

3. You feel that nothing seems to change

Let's take these one at a time.

Ending the darkness

The solution to feeling in the dark is getting information. The information you need is going to depend on the specific kind of power imbalance. You have to ask yourself, what information could the other person share with me that would make me feel more trust?

For example, Lisa realized that she'd be able to trust Brian a lot more if he shared with her what was going on with his business. He was surprised; he'd thought she wasn't interested. But then he started talking to her about their customers, their projects, the contracts they were bidding on. And the more Lisa knew about the business, the less powerful Brian seemed to her. He wasn't, she realized, doing what he wanted to do. *He was doing what he had to do.* And realizing this made her trust him a lot more.

Gaining influence

To counteract the feelings of helplessness, you need influence. I'm not talking about having a brother-in-law who is on the city council. In a relationship, influence just means that you feel your words carry weight and you have a reasonable chance of getting reasonable needs met.

The best way to get influence is to ask for it directly. Assuming the other person is not a power person, this will go far. It will certainly be far better than what Lisa had been doing, which was getting upset and yelling and crying. Sure, she sometimes got her way when she did that, but it just made the problem worse with Brian trying to figure out ways of gaining power in the face of her powerful emotions. And, like most people, the best way he could come up with to do that was to withdraw from her and shut her out, so she ended up with even less information and influence than she'd had before.

But the solution that works is so simple. You just say something like, "With your schedule [or "your ability to argue," or "your money," or "your boss's pressure on you"] it's very hard for me to feel that I can get many of my needs met. I need to be able to say that I want something and that it's important to me and if I say that, you'll take it seriously and really talk about it with me."

Those are the key words: *This is important to me.* These words need to be a signal between the two of you that indicates the matter is serious, and his listening shows how important you are to the other. It doesn't mean you'll always get what you want. But it will mean that you can have a satisfying discussion in which you can trust that your needs will be heard.

It's all in the follow-through

One more thing: Information and influence are great but they're not enough. If you have all these discussions but nothing changes, you're still going to feel disempowered and the mistrust will remain. You need to actually carry out the agreements you make.

If the other person has agreed to share certain information with you, it's not enough to do it for a short period of time. He has to keep on doing it.

If you make agreements about things that you need, there has to be follow-through. It's this follow-through on the information and influence that rebuilds trust. After all, we trust people who do what they've agreed to do. It's as simple as that. That's why nothing is more important than follow-through when it comes to rebuilding trust.

As YOU'LL SEE in the following chapter, power imbalances are just one of the ways differences between people can create trust issues. There are a lot of differences between any two people, so of course there are a lot of trust issues out there.

14

Restoring Trust When There Are Differences

L ET'S SAY I'M home sick with a sore throat and out of the goodness of your heart you come over with a big pot of chicken soup for me. What a nice thing to do!

You heat up a bowl and bring it to me in bed. After I slurp down a spoonful or two you ask me how I like it. Because my throat hurts, I don't want to talk. So I make a sign. I raise my hand, palm facing out, fingers extended and touch the tip of my forefinger to the tip of my thumb.

And you respond by . . . what? Well, if you're an American, you smile or you say, "Oh, good." Because to you I've just made the "okay" sign, a sign that many Americans think is the universal sign for okay.

But if you're from, say, Brazil, you don't smile at all. You're hurt, offended, infuriated. There you were, bringing me soup because you'd heard I was sick, and you ask me how it is and I make a sign that says to you, "Fuck you." Because that's what that sign means to someone from Brazil.

If the kindly soup bringer were from Turkey or Venezuela, my friendly "okay" sign would be interpreted as, "You're a homosexual," but not in a nice way, if you know what I mean.

I was just trying to express appreciation, and look at the mess I just made!

So suppose I decided that I don't want to risk these problems—the "okay" sign is too risky, which is what I learned after alienating my Brazilian, Turkish, and Venezuelan friends. This time, when an Iranian friend comes by with chicken soup for me and asks me how I like it, I try to play it safe. I give her a big, hearty thumbs-up. But guess what? A look of hurt and fury fills her face and she walks out.

What did I do this time?

Sigh. It turns out that the American thumbs-up gesture, signaling friendly appreciation to us, means "Shove this up your ass" to an Iranian.

I don't want you to conclude from this that you shouldn't bring me chicken soup when I have a cold. I would appreciate it and I think our relationship could survive my attempts at saying thank you.

But there are two really important conclusions that come from this.

How Differences Create Mistrust

The first conclusion is obvious. Things have very different meanings for people depending on their backgrounds. And it's not just national backgrounds. Important differences also come from age, class, gender, education, religion, and even which region of the country you come from.

The other conclusion is less obvious but even more important. It's how we get into trouble. It's not differences that get us into trouble, it's thinking we're similar when we're not. It's not appreciating the real differences that really exist.

Now if you're in a relationship with someone, you'll probably sort out pretty quickly hand signals for "okay" and "Fuck you." But there are many other differences that go far deeper and create far more trouble.

Here's an example. During World War II, there were a lot of American soldiers stationed in England. Many of them started dating English women and that's where the trouble began, leading to tremendous feelings of mistrust and betrayal.

It all came about because for the American GIs, kissing was something you did with a girl when you started to like each other. For the British women, kissing was a sign that you were pretty much engaged. Imagine the problems. You'd have an American boy pushing to get a kiss on the first or second date and the English girl resisting because for her it was far too early in the relationship. But eventually she would think, "Wow, this guy really loves me and wants to marry me. Maybe I should say yes." So she'd kiss him.

And here's where the feelings of betrayal came in. After that kiss all these English girls were thinking they were engaged. But the GIs might start dating another girl or head off to their next assignment without saying a word because to them it had been only a casual relationship.

The British women felt betrayed and abandoned, to the point where some of them committed suicide.

Again, it's not the difference that's the big problem, it's the not allowing for the difference. And you feel so betrayed because you *think* you know what something means.

THE SIZE OF THE PROBLEM. Do you think differences between people are a big problem when it comes to betrayal and mistrust in relationships?

They are a *huge* problem. It's a mark, really, of how far we've come from being a traditional society. In a traditional society, almost everyone marries someone from almost the identical background. In our society, not so much. Today, significant differences in background are the norm rather than the exception. After all, our society is so diverse and we are so mobile.

To take just one factor alone, many of us end up marrying someone we met in college, but many colleges are melting pots of people from quite different backgrounds. Of course, this can create a wonderfully productive and stimulating cross-pollination. But it too often becomes a risk factor leading to mistrust.

Erin and Kevin

I'm thinking about one young couple I recently worked with. They were both ethnically Irish, but other than that they couldn't

have been more different. Erin was a working-class Roman Cath-
olic Irish immigrant from a Dublin slum. Kevin was upper-class
New England Episcopalian boarding-school Irish from a tony
Boston suburb.

They came to me in deep trouble. Erin, according to Kevin,
was crazy with jealousy. Wherever they went, she would accuse
him of flirting. When they went to a party, afterward she would
scream at him for hitting on all the women there. She would accuse him of trying to make dates with them. He would deny it,
and she would accuse him of being a liar. Soon they stopped
going to parties.

Their life was turning into hell. Not surprisingly, this precipitated a huge crisis of trust, which polarized them to the point
where she was accusing him of being a pig who was trying to
sleep with half the women they knew. And he accused her of
being an idiot peasant from the middle ages.

What was the problem? Was Erin just a nut? Was she just
paranoid? Before I concluded that it was all Erin's problem, I
checked into the differences in their background.

Well, guess what? In Kevin's world, men and women mixed
freely both socially and in the workplace, and they chatted,
teased, and flirted with each other all the time, even if they were
in relationships with other people. Erin came from a world in
which men and women kept themselves pretty separate from one
another. At parties, the men would talk to the men, the women
to the women, and that was that.

The more I explored their backgrounds with them, the more
it became clear to me—and to them—that Erin wasn't a nut at
all. No more than a Brazilian is nutty for thinking that what we
call the "okay" sign means fuck you. But the problem wasn't just

that there were deep differences between them. It was that they didn't suspect that these differences existed. It's not knowing where the landmines are that blow people up.

DEALING WITH DIFFERENCES

So what do you do about this if you're dealing with mistrust in your relationship?

These days, I assume that in almost every relationship affected by mistrust some of it—maybe a lot of it, maybe most of it—is caused by the ways the two people are different from each other and by the fact that they're not aware of those differences.

For example, when my husband and I first got married we saw eye to eye on so many things and shared so many similar tastes that we thought we were as alike as two peas in a pod. Many couples go through a period feeling like this. Often when two people are falling in love a phrase they'll use a lot is "Me, too!" See how similar we are! Isn't it wonderful!

This is great, and it may be true, but it can also be very harmful. My husband and I would get into fights where he'd accuse me of overreacting to something and I'd accuse him of not caring. But because we had this myth of similarity, we didn't see where these fights really came from. The fact is that our family backgrounds were very different. Things were always operatic and hysterical in my family. You were never hot. You were boiling. On fire. In his family, they were understated instead of overstated. You were never hot. Instead you'd say something like, "Do you think it's a little warm in here?"

And that was another thing. In my family, everyone was very direct. Too direct, probably. In his family, everyone was indirect.

We were speaking different languages even though we thought we were speaking the same language. And it made us mistrust each other. He thought I was power mad. I thought he was in hiding.

FINDING THE HIDDEN DIFFERENCES. This is one of those problems that feel impossible to solve when you don't realize what's going on, but pretty easy to solve when you do. And so the solution begins, step one, with just acknowledging the fact that there is a difference in your backgrounds that may be causing the disagreement and mistrust.

How do you find these differences in backgrounds?

Well, you have to talk to each other. Work your way through this list of questions:

How is it that you keep getting into the same fight?
This question is key. If differences between you are causing mistrust, then those differences are going to keep coming up and you're going to keep having the same fight. But to answer this question, you can't be playing the blame game. You'll know you're on the right track when your answer has a balance between what one of you thinks and what the other thinks. Something like, "We keep getting into fights because you seem too intense to me, which makes you seem like a nut, and I seem too laid back to you, which makes me seem like I either don't care or I'm in hiding."

What differences in your backgrounds might account for these differences?

You see, what you're trying to do here is separate what the other person does that's hurtful from who the other person is. If I offended my Brazilian neighbor by making a sign that she thought meant fuck you, then if she understands the differences in our backgrounds and what that sign means to me, she'll know that I didn't want to offend her. If I understand that my husband's laid-back manner is just something he learned in his family, then I'll know that it's just how he is. It doesn't mean he's in hiding or doesn't care.

So what are some other examples of differences in background that led people to become mistrustful of another person?

Will and Molly

Will was a painter, a real artist, the kind whose work only hoity-toity art critics claimed to understand. His second wife, Molly, worked in the coffee shop where he went every morning. She was a simple, happy, friendly soul, refreshingly free of the artistic bullshit he so often encountered. In fact, she knew nothing about art.

After they got married, Will started making sketches of her, and that's where the trouble began. These were not pretty pictures. They showed every wart and blemish, every sag and pouch and wrinkle that Molly had and a few that she didn't yet have. Molly was furious, and more. She accused Will of a plot to humiliate her and destroy her self-confidence. "Why did you marry me if you think I'm so ugly? Why did you marry me if you just wanted to destroy me?"

Will tried to explain that phony artists made pretty pictures. Real artists pursued a vision.

"So your vision is wanting to make people think you hate me and that I'm ugly?" Poor Molly.

Poor Will. He hauled out a bunch of art books and tried to show her paintings by artists like Picasso, Matisse, Lucien Freud, Francis Bacon, and many others who liked or loved their models and yet . . . look at what they painted!

These great works of art cut no ice with Molly. "Well then, you're all a bunch of women-hating motherfuckers," she explained.

Molly said that if he loved her he would make a picture of her that made her look pretty. Will said that he would never violate his artistic integrity. Molly asked what the difference was between artistic integrity and being an asshole.

They finally hit on a solution. He just wouldn't ever draw her. But the damage had been done. Molly could never shake the feeling that Will thought she was hideous. He was haunted by the feeling that he, a real artist, had made a terrible mistake in marrying a woman who couldn't begin to appreciate his work.

And yet over time there was healing. As long as he wasn't drawing her, he acted like a man who loved his wife, Molly thought. And she started learning about art and developed a real appreciation of what artists were trying to do, especially modern artists, who typically felt that art wasn't about beauty and certainly not about making pretty pictures. It was about the truth of a particular vision, although it never reached the point of her appreciating his pictures of her.

And this healing happened because they were able to see what the differences between them really were all about.

ACCEPTING DIFFERENCES. There's one last mistake to avoid, and this will make your life a lot easier. Dealing with differences doesn't mean becoming the same. So don't make the mistake of trying to turn one of you into the other.

If one of you is a Jew and the other is a Christian, for example, it might be convenient if one or the other converted, but it's not necessary if your goal is to prevent feelings of hurt and betrayal. All you have to do with this or any other difference is *understand* and *accept* where the other is coming from. You don't have to agree. That's the key point. The Jew doesn't have to agree that Jesus is the Son of God. And Will doesn't have to agree that an artist should draw pretty pictures of his wife.

You just have to do something much easier: talk about what things mean to you so the other person understands and accepts the difference.

You might be wondering: Really? Just understanding where the differences are and where they come from can solve everything?

Sadly, no. People usually get along precisely because they have similar tastes and preferences. If I know that two people don't like the same food or the same movies or the same TV shows or the same people, then it's going to make me wonder how they can have a successful relationship. They'll either be very distant or they'll be quarrelling all the time.

But this is not a general book about how to have a happy relationship. It's about how to heal mistrust. And you heal mistrust by uncovering hidden differences and by arriving at an understanding of where those differences come from.

By itself, healing mistrust won't remove differences and it won't protect a relationship from differences that drive two people apart. But it's still enormously valuable to heal mistrust. Mistrust is usually a much bigger problem in relationships than differences.

THERE'S ONE KIND of difference that we haven't touched on here because it requires special handling. It's when there's a difference between the two of you about how hidden or open you want to be. Whenever one person is more open than the other, the groundwork is laid for a lot of suspicion. And that's what we're going to deal with next.

15

Being Open vs. Being Hidden

IN MAY 2010, Jimmy, a forty-four-year-old software engineer, lost his job. It was a bad time to be laid off, with the unemployment rate rising and software jobs being exported overseas. It was a particularly bad time for Jimmy and his family. His oldest kid had just started high school, so college costs were looming, and a contractor had just started adding a family room to their house.

Jimmy was scared, and, even worse, he felt terrible about himself. He shouldn't have let himself become one of those people who lost their job, he thought. He shouldn't have put his family in this situation.

And he didn't know how to tell his wife, Laura, about this. He was afraid of her fear and anger. So for many days Jimmy left his house at the usual time every morning, supposedly to go to work. But in fact he ran errands, went to the library to start organizing his job search, hung out at coffee shops, and spent a lot of time just driving around. It was while he was driving around town that Laura saw him one day at 3:30 in the afternoon. When he came home that evening, supposedly from work, she asked him what he'd been doing that afternoon on Route 20 near the Burlington Mall.

That's when he confessed that he'd lost his job four weeks earlier. This confession shook Laura like an earthquake. "Why didn't you tell me sooner?" she demanded with angry tears pouring down her cheeks. "Why didn't you trust me?" On and on Laura went, raging at feeling betrayed by his mistrust. Then, before Jimmy could catch his breath, Laura started launching into, "What else aren't you telling me? How many other secrets do you have?"

The structure of their love seemed to collapse around her. It wasn't just about his hiding his being laid off. As Laura later realized, that structure had been seriously weakened by other trust issues. Laura had always been suspicious, always expecting to have the rug pulled out from under her, because she'd always experienced Jimmy as being hidden. And Jimmy, too, had never trusted Laura because he'd seen her as someone who "overreacted" (his word) to any bad news.

It's normal. I now see, after much research and clinical experience, that theirs is not an unusual marriage. And that's because it has known a good share of everyday betrayals and mistrust. Nothing worthy of a news headline happened, like a sexual affair. There was just enough hurt to make them feel distant and unsafe. Just enough hurt to throw a pall over the possibility of affection. Just enough hurt to weaken things so that when Laura found out that her husband didn't trust her enough to tell her he'd been laid off, the whole relationship seemed to collapse in a heap of mistrust.

Right now Jimmy and Laura's marriage is in critical condition. It can only be saved if they face the dynamic they're caught in, where he seems hidden to her and yet she makes it hard for him to be more open. This dynamic is quite common. People are constantly delaying giving bad news to people they're close to.

Think of all the people, for example, whose doctor told them they have a terrible disease but who didn't tell their partner right away, maybe because they wanted time to process the information, or maybe because they wanted to enjoy a few days or weeks with their loved one without the relationship being clouded by this news. And of course it's perfectly natural when there's any delay in anyone telling you something or when someone doesn't tell the whole story at first, for you to wonder what else is being hidden.

One Person Always Seems More Hidden

It's amazing. I've seen it over and over. You can have two open people. In their previous relationships they were both the more open partner. But now they're in a new relationship, and watch what happens.

Inevitably, in this new relationship, because two people are never identical, one will be more open than the other. Then guess what? By a kind of weird black magic, one person's being relatively less open soon starts to look to his partner as his being hidden. It's always like this. No matter how open a person I am, if you think I'm less open than you are, you're going to think I'm hiding things from you and so you're going to think I'm hidden. This dynamic always leads to trust issues. In most cases these are small, easily dealt with trust issues. But one partner seeming hidden to the other always has the potential to break out into a serious sense of betrayal.

HIDDENNESS AND MISTRUST. Here's how hiddenness creates trust issues. People can hide but they can rarely hide their hiding. You might not know what I'm not telling you, but if I seem like a hidden person, you will have a very strong feeling that I'm withholding something. But I wouldn't be hiding something good, would I? So you must think that I'm hiding something that could hurt you in some way. And since you don't know what it is, it could be anything. At that point, every part of life with me becomes a danger for you, and mistrust becomes a blanket response.

Let's look at how this plays out. If I'm less open than you and you push on me to open up—and you will!—I'll just withdraw all the more. You see, no one thinks of themselves as being too hidden. I'm going to think of myself as being as open as I can or want to be. So if you push on me further, I'm going to feel probed, penetrated, and invaded. I'll resist. I'll put up barriers.

You'll find it very frustrating. Soon we're likely to fall into a state of angry polarization where the more you push, the more I keep hiding. (Or you might just give up. Tired of pushing me to be open, you might become closed yourself. Then the relationship descends into a kind of ice age.)

Here's another dynamic. Once someone sees you as hidden, it can be hard to prove that you're not holding something back, no matter how open you believe you've become. After all, the mind has so many dark and winding paths it's impossible to prove there's not something hidden there.

So in most relationships there's one person desperately hungry for more openness. That person is usually feeling very mistrustful. So, it turns out, is his partner.

I know this intimately. I've lived it.

My story, continued

I was only four when my mother brought my brother and me to New York from Europe. We were penniless refugees. Before we left Europe, I'd had a father. Imagine my surprise when my mother and brother and I got on the boat and he didn't come with us. My mother kept their breakup a secret from us until the very last minute.

Once we got settled in New York, I kept pestering my mother to get me a new father so I could be like all the other little girls. One day she shipped me off to a friend's house for the afternoon. When I was brought back to our apartment there was my mother announcing, "You have a new father." She'd gotten married that afternoon. I'd had no idea.

Growing up, there was a lot of that in my family. Some of it was my mother being who she was. But most of it, I think, came from the fact that she was very old country, and in the old country grownups didn't discuss with little kids what they were going to do.

Growing up in a family like that, with so much secrecy, guess how I felt about wanting the people close to me to be open?

Did you guess that I wanted people close to me to be open, to save me from awful secrets? Well, if you guessed that, you were *wrong*! Not completely wrong. There was always a part of me that demanded that anyone close to me be completely open. But there was another part of me. So many of the secrets that had come flying out of the closet when I was a kid had been bad news. So while I wanted people close to me to be open, I didn't want them to reveal anything hard for me to deal with.

And that's the fundamental issue people struggle with below the surface when there's conflict over hiddenness and openness.

MY POOR HUSBAND. I'd always known I liked people close to me to be open. But it's taken me my whole life to realize that as much as I want openness, I also fear it. To be precise, I want people to be completely open with me but to only share good news. Especially people in my family. Super especially, my husband.

My poor husband. He is definitely not as open a person as I am. So of course I think of him as being hidden. But does he think of himself as being hidden? Not at all. Far from it. He actually thinks of himself as quite open. It's just that he likes to "think about" things before he shares them. This can mean thinking about things for a year or more before he shares it, because he hasn't gotten his thoughts perfectly sorted out yet.

So he's open, all right, just not with the raw process.

And what do I do? I get on his case for being so hidden, and then I proceed to flip out over the news flashes he decides to share with me.

My clinical work and research show me that almost everyone is like this. We're frightened by hiddenness, but we're also frightened by what crawls out from that hiddenness into the sunlight.

And so we give the message: Don't keep anything from me, but don't tell me anything I don't want to hear. And this makes the people around us crazy.

A Solvable Problem

This is a very solvable problem, but you have to understand what the real problem is.

Of course, some people are really very hidden. Getting any information from them is as hard as a hobo getting a good table at a fine restaurant. And if someone is a hidden person, period, and if you need to be with someone who is open, then you don't have a trust problem, you have a compatibility problem. And it's not one you'll probably solve. Hidden people just stay hidden. In this case, you might have to move on from this relationship.

But most of the time, the prognosis is much better. The other person isn't essentially hidden at all. Maybe he's a little more hidden than you are, but so what? The real problem isn't the other person. And it's not you, either. It's the two of you. You're at an impasse. It can be resolved, but first we have to understand it.

Angela and David

When Angela and David met, she'd recently broken up with her ex. David was a little concerned about this as he started getting closer to her, but she promised him that her previous relationship was completely over. One day months later, though, after David and Angela's relationship had gotten really serious, David noticed that she had left her laptop open when she went to take a shower. He casually glanced at the screen and noticed that Angela was in the middle of answering an email from her ex. David couldn't resist snooping. As he went through her email, he saw that she had been maintaining a very friendly relationship with this ex.

So it wasn't *over* over. Perhaps it wasn't over at all. David felt lied to and, possibly, betrayed.

When she came out of the shower, he asked her about the email. To David's surprise, they ended up having a huge fight about his being a snoop. She showed him the whole email chain and demanded that he find something that even "his evil little mind" could find incriminating. David had to admit there was nothing incriminating in those emails.

"Besides," Angela said, "I've always been friendly with my exes. I'm sure I'll be friendly with you when you're an ex, which at this rate you're going to end up being pretty soon."

The fight blew over, but not the issue. And here's what ended up happening. It's not what anyone wanted to happen, but when hiddenness and mistrust become an issue in relationships, it's what too often does happen.

Angela was not a hidden person. In fact, she prided herself on being very open. After all, she was the one who'd left her computer open with the email up on the screen for everyone to see.

But something happened to her when David responded to it the way he did. *She* stopped trusting *him*. If he was going to get nutty with every little revelation, maybe he was a guy for whom her being open was more trouble than it was worth. She thought of Jack Nicholson's line in *A Few Good Men*, "You can't *handle* the truth."

And of course he didn't feel he could trust her anymore either. It's not that she'd betrayed him. He had to admit that those emails were perfectly innocent. It was that she'd kept something from him. And that's how the worm of doubt entered his brain. It always leads to this terrible, destructive question: "If she kept *that* from me, what else is she keeping from me?"

They became locked in a tragic process that's as hard to get out of as a pit of quicksand. The more he thought she was hidden, the more he snooped. The more he snooped, the more she hid.

It's always like this when someone feels the other person is hidden. If you're with someone who you think is hiding things from you, it's humanly impossible not to try to pry them open. The snooping doesn't have to include hunting for secret email accounts and getting into your partner's phone to see who they've called. It might simply take the form of asking endless questions in a hurt, prying, accusing tone, or pouncing on any seeming contradiction in what the other person said.

The point is that if you don't trust me because you think I'm hidden, I will end up not trusting you because I think you won't be able to deal with whatever it is I'm hiding.

It's an impasse. So how do you get out of it?

GETTING THROUGH THE IMPASSE. To end this horrible, destructive, unnecessary state of suspicion, the place you want to get to is a simple agreement:

"I'll open up if you won't slam me."

"I won't slam you if you open up."

I know what you might be thinking. "Why do I have to agree to anything? I'm not the one who's hidden. He's hidden. All he has to do is open up. Stop hiding things. That's it."

I've felt the same way myself. There are two ways to approach problems between two people. One is the legal approach. You find a judge who determines blame, issues a ruling, and imposes a remedy. "You, Mr. Jones," the judge says, pounding his gavel down, "started this by being hidden and now you have to be open. Case closed."

And you know what? This is what we all really want deep down. When I have a problem with my husband, I don't want therapy. Therapy means talk and work and I'm tired of talking and working. I want a judge to fly down from the sky, point a bony finger at my husband, find him guilty, tell him what to do to make things right from now, and fly away. No muss, no fuss!

That's what we want, *but we can't get it.* There aren't any judges like this. And even if there were, just try getting the other person to accept a guilty verdict. I know I wouldn't accept his verdict if it turned out to be me the judge was pointing his bony finger at.

THE THERAPEUTIC ROUTE. So we have to go the therapeutic route. It has two great virtues. It's all we have. And it really works.

The therapeutic approach says this: Okay, you knuckleheads. I don't know who started this and I don't care. All I know is that right now you're in a state of mutual mistrust. And you're both going to have to do something to get out of it.

What I said to David and Angela was that basically she would have to start being more open and he would have to stop getting nutty every time she came out with some little revelation.

It sounds easy, but it's not. The person who's hidden has to swallow her fears and take a risk, hoping that this time she won't be slammed for revealing some nugget. It's hard to confess when you risk anger or the third degree.

And it's hard for the other person, too. The fact is that when two people's lives are connected, there are all kinds of things going for each one that will be upsetting for the other.

"You thought I liked your mother, but I don't."

Or, "I've been pretending that it doesn't bother me that you're bald, but it does."

Or, "I get really depressed sometimes and I haven't wanted to tell you."

Or, "I was telling the truth when I said that I don't want to have more children, but now I've changed my mind."

Or, "It's actually not okay with me that you go off and play golf all day Saturday, but I don't say anything because I don't want to have a fight about it."

ENCOURAGING OPENNESS. It's hard not to get upset when we hear things like this. And we usually make two mistakes. We get upset at what the other person has revealed. And we give the other person the third degree about when they first knew this and why they didn't tell us sooner and what else are they hiding. Just think about this for a moment: The other person has just been open, and now he's feeling slammed for being hidden. That's bad psychology.

If you want to encourage openness, you don't slam someone

for being hidden when they've just been open. Because if you do, they're likely to think, Why bother?

And it's probably not wise to get upset about what they have to say, because, again, they're likely to feel, Why bother?

You see, that's *why* we're hidden. We don't want to face a shitstorm when we reveal whatever it is we have to reveal.

David was really upset when I talked to him about this. "So you're telling me that if I want Angela to be open, I have to be like, oh, whatever you say, that's fine?"

Notice how open David was with me about his dismay with my advice. All my patients are open with me. Why do you think that's the case? It's because I don't freak out on them! People don't want to be freaked out on and so they are not going to be open if they're going to face a freak-out. In fact, let's face it, they're not going to be open unless what they face is real acceptance. *My acceptance is what unlocks the door to your openness.* That's the deal.

But David had a point. In fairy-tale land, we can respond to anything anyone has to say with acceptance. In real life, some things are upsetting and hard to accept. How could David not be upset, for example, if Angela told him she didn't like his being bald. How could he not feel insulted, rejected, and betrayed (since she'd sort of led him to believe that she was fine with his baldness)?

CAN WE EVER ACHIEVE TOTAL OPENNESS? Then David hit on an even deeper issue. "Wait a minute," he said. "are you telling me that if I want Angela to be open about what's going on with her, I have to go into hiding with my real response? Aren't you then saying that someone always has to be in hiding?"

Touché! At least it would be touché if I didn't have a really good solution to this.

You see, I used to get into the same thing with my husband. He'd reveal something to me. I'd get all shook up, and then he'd be sorry he opened his mouth. So he'd go into hiding again. I'd bug him about that. He'd make some little trial revelation, and I'd flip out again. By "flip out," I'm not just talking about screaming and going crazy. It could be that I'd get upset. It could be that I'd get quiet and withdrawn. It could be that I'd just ask a lot of uncomfortable questions.

So why do I call this "flipping out"? Because when anyone has been in hiding about something, they're feeling vulnerable. The only response they really want, if we're at all honest with ourselves, is something like, "Oh, that's okay," or "Don't worry. I understand."

So how do you give that when you don't feel it?

What I've found that works almost like magic is letting the other person know that you really, really *want* to give them to feel you welcome their openness. (If you can't think of anything else, just say, "I really welcome your openness, and I'm grateful for it, even though I'm not happy about what you've said.") For some reason, just knowing that the other person knows how vulnerable you are makes you feel safer.

BEING HONEST ABOUT WHAT WE WANT. Let's say, for example, that a guy comes to his wife and says, awkwardly, that he wonders if she's thought about spicing up their sex life by having a threesome. It wouldn't surprise anyone if she got upset. "What the hell is wrong with you? What makes you think I'd ever want to get involved with something disgusting like that."

But what has she just done? One thing she's done is perfectly okay. She's said no. There's nothing wrong with saying no if that's how you feel. But the other thing she's done is totally against her own self-interest, unless her self-interest involves shutting down any adventure and creativity in their sex lives, to say nothing of shutting down his being open.

Her husband—let's call him Bozo, because somehow I think he is a Bozo—won't think, "Oh, I guess she's really not open to that but I bet she's open to all kinds of other things." Instead, Bozo will think, "Well, that's the last time I'm going to share one of my ideas with her." And their plain-vanilla sex lives will turn that much plainer.

We have to be ruthlessly honest with ourselves about what we want. If we just react to things, then that means we've lost complete control over getting what we want in life. But if we're driven by what we want, then we have a good chance of getting it. If this woman wants to have a vibrant, open, and exciting sex life with her husband, then if Bozo says to his wife that he wonders if she's open to trying a threesome, she'd better not throw the baby out with the bathwater. Otherwise he won't share any of his adventurous ideas in the future.

What she needs to say is something like, "I'm so glad you shared that with me. [Remember: welcoming a suggestion is very different from agreeing to it.] I love it that you feel comfortable enough to take a risk and share some adventurous ideas with me. As for this particular idea, I have to say that it's just not for me. But I hope you'll keep bringing fresh ideas to me. The more, the better."

You see the principle. First, you welcome the effort. You welcome the openness. Second, feel free to say no to the suggestion itself. You don't have to let yourself feel pressured. After all, even if the other person is pressuring you, you're still free to say no. But it's not smart to shut down the other person's sharing of ideas. So, third, repeat your gratitude for and openness to the other person's being open.

AND THAT'S HOW you heal the mistrust that grows when one of you has been hidden. **You can't command openness, but you can reward it.** And you can reward it even if you don't go along with the specific idea contained in what the other person is saying.

Just remember to use what I call "the sandwich." Your meat is your response to what the other person actually said. The bread on either side is your responding positively to the other person's being open. So appreciate the openness. Then deal calmly with the content of what he's saying or asking. And then conclude by again appreciating the openness.

The real secret is that people want to be open. They're hungry for closeness. It's lonely otherwise. It's just that they feel trapped by their own hiddenness. And so they are always making little attempts to show themselves, like a Victorian lady lifting her skirt just enough to show a bit of ankle. To reduce their hiddenness, what you have to do is be alert for these little revelations and make sure you welcome them.

It's the job of us more open people to encourage hidden people to be more open. With a little bit of encouragement, they will be.

16

The Impact of Past Betrayals

THEY SAY THAT when you sleep with someone you're sleeping with all the people *they've* slept with. I don't know how far back to take this. Does it mean that I've possibly slept with Abraham Lincoln and Henry the Eighth? But I get the point. And in the same way, it's also true that when you get involved with someone you have to deal with all the betrayals they've experienced from everyone they were involved with before you.

You may never have betrayed anyone yourself. But somehow you are implicated in betrayal anyway. If a guy starts dating a woman whose previous boyfriend used to beat her, that new guy is going to have to deal with the woman's fear of his beating her.

This can feel terribly unfair. But it's very common, more so today than ever. People are getting married later than before, having been in more relationships before they marry. The people we marry have not only been around the block a bunch of times, they've gotten run over a few times, too.

Just think about it. By the time the average girl, for example, is eighteen she's had her heart broken at least once by some boy and has been painfully betrayed by one of her friends. There's no counting how many stories she's heard about similar experiences. She's most probably lived through a divorce, whether her parents' or that of a relative or a close friend's parents. And it's pretty much the same for men. I know this because I've asked men and women when they first learned that trust was going to be a trouble spot in their lives. It usually starts at eighteen or earlier.

And if that's what it's like at eighteen, imagine what this is like by the time people are twenty-eight and then thirty-eight and then forty-eight, and so on. With every year we accumulate more intimate knowledge of all the ways people let each other down. Maybe we've done some of the letting down ourselves.

Think about what this does to us.

Tracy

Just this past year, Tracy, a woman in her forties, sat across from me and asked me with the most piercing expression, "Answer this question—and whether or not I kill myself depends on your answer: Will I ever be able to trust a man again?"

Tracy was divorced. Her ex-husband had betrayed her by not being the man she thought he was. He'd turned out to be selfish and critical instead of generous and supportive. Then she'd fallen in love with a man . . . well, "love" isn't quite the word for it. It was, according to her, a relationship of spectacular depth and intimacy and passion. They felt, she said, connected as no two people had ever been connected. That they would share their lives and futures seemed incontestable.

And then he dumped her. A bolt from the blue if there ever was one, sending her into a suicidal depression. Her question to me, sad as it was, and putting aside the threat of suicide, made sense. How *would* she ever trust a man again?

A DIFFERENT PERSPECTIVE. Let's look at this from a different perspective for a moment. Suppose Tracy one day did decide to take another chance on love. What do you think it would feel like to be that new guy?

It would be rough, don't you think? I'm sure Tracy is going to do what everyone in her situation does: keep the person she gets involved with next at arm's length until she trusts him, except that she never will trust him. She'll always be waiting for the other shoe to drop. Tired of waiting for a feeling of trust that never comes, she'll want to accelerate the process. If she can somehow put him to the test, then maybe she'll feel safer. So she'll do to him what manufacturers do with a piece of equipment that needs to be used in a very heavy-duty environment. She'll put him through every challenge she can think of.

And then what do you think will happen? You and I both know the answer. If he likes her enough, he'll hang in there while she puts him through his paces, being as difficult as possible. She'll get angry with him over little things. She'll be fickle. She'll be distant. She'll be a handful. But at some point he's going to get sick of the difficulties and break things off. And then she'll feel validated that indeed you can't trust any guy.

It can also play out in a very different way. Instead of holding him at arm's length, she can hold herself at arm's length. Instead of being difficult, she can just not be *there*. Sure, they'll go through the motions as far as anyone can see. As far as he can see, it's a normal, developing relationship.

But what no one can see, maybe not even Tracy herself, is that she's put her heart on ice. This may seem like a perfectly lovely relationship, she says to herself, but I can't trust it any further than I can throw it, so I'll go along as if this relationship were happening to someone else. This is a safe but horrible strategy. It's safe because you're immune from getting hurt. It's horrible because you can never feel any of the good stuff when you're keeping your heart locked in its own private refrigerator.

THE MOST COMMON PATTERN. The most common pattern these days is a combination of these two ways for things to play out.

Most of us don't like to present ourselves as victims of betrayal when we're just getting to know someone. On the first few dates, probably neither of you will drag out your stories of the ways you've been betrayed. And even if you do, you'll probably soft-pedal your rage and mistrust.

This means that both people are vulnerable. I, with my mistrust, am vulnerable to being hurt by you. But you're also vulnerable to being hurt by me if you innocently do something that somehow stimulates my mistrust. All this is a serious risk factor for our being able to get together.

No wonder there is a distant or prickly quality to so many relationships. People aren't walking on eggshells. They're walking on the dry, brittle bones of past betrayals. This is the heart-on-ice phase.

Then at some point, out of nowhere, comes the phase where

you climb out of the closet and see if the other person can handle the real you.

Now you can see how the ways we've been hurt in previous relationships can make a big mess in our current one.

SOLUTIONS

How in the world do you deal with this? How can you ever find both safety and love if you or your partner has been hurt before?

Jeff and Amanda

Jeff and Amanda came to work with me. Jeff had gotten sick of how difficult Amanda was making things, and Amanda was sick of Jeff's being sick of her.

Here's how they got into this mess.

Amanda was the kind of pretty young woman who, you would think, could have her pick of boyfriends. Well, she must have had pretty poor judgment because she sure picked a lot of losers. During her twenties, Amanda had been with guys who dumped her, rejected her, turned into druggies, or became abusive. And now she was sick of being hurt. Amanda never wanted to be hurt again.

Poor Amanda. But poor Jeff, too. When he first met her, he thought he'd found the perfect woman. Little did he suspect.

For the first six months of their relationship, Amanda played the role of the loving girlfriend. Jeff couldn't see that this was a protective mask. Amanda was playing a role so if that young woman got hurt, the real Amanda would remain untouched.

After six months, though, Amanda sensed that Jeff just might be okay. There were no danger signs. And that scared the crap out of her. If he seemed safe, then she'd have to go forward with the relationship and if she went forward with the relationship there might be some "real" Jeff who would come leaping out of the darkness and hurt her terribly.

All Amanda could do—all most people think of doing—is put Jeff to the test in the hope of proving his reliability.

THE NEW AMANDA. Suddenly his sweet girl Amanda was gone. This new Amanda started giving him a hell of a time. She was angry, demanding, judgmental, suspicious. Even Amanda didn't know what had come over her, and Jeff certainly didn't. And that's when they came to work with me.

At first Amanda couldn't say why she was like this. But then I met with her one on one and it soon all came out. To me it was obvious. How could someone who had been so hurt so often not try to make herself feel safe by doing the things Amanda was doing? She really had two goals.

One was to act scary. She was, in effect, doing to Jeff what most people do to their partner after they've been betrayed by them. It was a kind of pre-betrayal reign of terror, just to serve as a warning.

The other thing Amanda was doing was making a test. Guys had dumped her and abandoned her in the past. How could she count on Jeff to stay true to her unless she knew he could withstand this onslaught? If he stayed with her when she was being awful, then surely he wouldn't leave her when she went back to being good.

Most people who've been hurt in the past like Amanda do

some version of what she did with Jeff. But it never gives them the protection they'd hoped for. In some cases, it destroys relationships that might well have survived without this stress. At a minimum, it introduces a sour note that's hard to recover from. And of course it provides no protection at all against other forms of betrayal.

But we're all like Amanda. We don't do what's best. We do what pops into our heads.

A WAY OUT. Fortunately, in their case it wasn't too late yet. They both needed to know what was going on. Jeff was not particularly relieved at hearing the explanation for her behavior. He said to me, "So . . . given what she's been through, does this mean that I'm in for this kind of testing for the rest of my life?"

He put his finger on the problem. This is an issue we've seen before. It's the old battle between safety and trust, how when we can't trust, the things we do to feel safe usually damage our relationships.

But the good news is that no one has to stay stuck in this pattern. There are ways out of it. And that's what I helped Jeff and Amanda find.

They each needed their own form of help. Amanda needed what everyone who's been hurt in previous relationships needs: a way to trust without doing things that damage the relationship. And that means one thing: finding an alternative to what they've been doing that doesn't work.

I helped Amanda see what her tactics of keeping her heart cased in ice and of putting her partner through an ordeal really meant. They were, of course, perfectly understandable. There's a powerful emotional logic to these tactics. Just think about it:

If you have an old rickety chair that might collapse when you sit on it, you either won't sit on it at all or you'll jump up and down on it just to make sure it won't fall apart.

But there is a third alternative that works beautifully, far better than the other two. Let's go back to that rickety old chair. Not sitting on it at all just deprives you of any benefit from the chair. Jumping up and down on it pretty much guarantees that what you're afraid of will happen.

THE SMARTEST THING TO DO. What would be the smartest thing to do? You'd check it out as carefully as you can and then you'd sit on it as if it were a normal chair. That way it would have a chance of serving you well. And what if, in spite of everything, it one day collapsed under you? Well, that's a risk we all have to take. If it doesn't check out, you shouldn't sit on it. But if it does check out, sitting on it is far less likely to hurt you than jumping up and down on it.

And that's what I helped Amanda do. That's all any of us can do.

First, the checking out.

How *do* you check someone out? There's a lot you can do. Most of all, you can check out how the other person has been in the past. Here's how you do that. *You shouldn't let yourself get too involved with someone until you get to know their friends and family.* How can you know someone without seeing them interact with those people? How can you say you've done due diligence unless you've talked with people who've known him for a long time and casually inquired into what happened in his previous relationships? Those people are your informants.

If you take the time to check out the other person this way, you'll be amazed at what you'll find, good or bad. And by the way: Googling someone and visiting their Facebook page can sometimes be helpful here, but they can also be the result of careful self-presentation. The gold standard is the real people in the other person's life.

But you have to be prepared to walk away. Many people are experts at putting up a good front. No matter how good a person seems, if they don't pass the friends-and-family test, you've got to take a pass.

By the way: Taking the time to check someone out doesn't mean you have to put your heart on ice. One of the best ways to check someone out is to be vulnerable and be yourself, from the very beginning, if at all possible. You can only say you know the real other person when you can say that he knows the real you.

Next, going forward as if you trust the other person.

In truth, you don't completely trust the other person because you've been hurt badly in the past. I get it. But you've got to understand that your least bad alternative here is your best alternative. And our instinctive tendency to either put our heart on ice or subject the other person to abusive testing are pretty bad alternatives. Going forward with a hopeful heart puts you at risk, but it's still the least risky way to go.

It's not as if you were alone in this. I've worked with countless people who have been hurt in previous relationships. *I* was pretty badly hurt in previous relationships before I married. But if you look at what actually works to help people find love, the only good alternative is trusting and moving forward.

WHEN YOU WANT TO BE TRUSTED

But what if you're involved with someone who's been hurt in the past?

You have to be starkly honest with yourself. If you're with someone who in the past was hurt more than most, you might be in for some tough sledding. This is not going to be a maintenance-free relationship. Even if the other person has heeded my advice not to put you through an ordeal, there's still going to be some of that. Plus there's going to be less margin for error when you screw up. And we all screw up.

So you have to ask yourself if the other person is worth it. *Do that now* before you get in any deeper. And if you realize it's not worth it, don't hesitate to leave. People often make a huge and terrible mistake here. They're with someone who's been hurt, and so they don't want to hurt them anymore. So they stay even though they want to leave. This just makes things worse. The inevitable breakup will happen; it's just that now you'll use up months or years of the other person's life and hurt them even more.

If you decide that the other person *is* worth it—yes, he's been badly hurt before, but he's smart, sane, charming, and attractive—here are some rules to follow that will heal the other person's mistrust.

By the way: You should follow these rules whenever you're in a situation where you want to earn the other person's trust.

Don't mess up.

Yes, I know, you're not perfect. No one expects you to be. But think about this analogy: Suppose you went to a restaurant and found a bug in your salad. Yikes! You raised a ruckus and management was very apologetic and didn't charge you for your meal. Then let's say you decided to give them another chance and go back a couple of weeks later. Wouldn't you be hoping they would recognize you and make an extra effort to make sure that nothing goes wrong?

Well, why should it be any different for the people in our lives. They know that you know that they've been hurt. So they just want you to make an extra effort not to hurt them again.

What kinds of things am I talking about? Nothing all that unusual. Just things like not forgetting the person's birthday. Not coming home late without a heads up. Not saying mean things. Not checking out other women when you're out with her. And don't forget to ask what you can do to show that you care about not hurting her.

This is not about being perfect. We all make mistakes. So, okay, make your share of mistakes. But if you want to earn someone's trust, especially when she's been hurt in the past, avoid making the big mistakes.

Don't lie or be hidden.

I've noticed something very interesting: People who've been hurt in previous relationships often think that the person they're with now is a liar. Why is that? Is it perhaps just paranoia?

No. I believe that people who've been hurt in previous relationships are more likely to be lied to by their current partner. And here's why.

If you're in a relationship with someone who's been hurt a lot, she's going to be very vulnerable. But you, like everyone else, are very imperfect. And what do you think happens when Mr. Imperfect meets Ms. Vulnerable? Explosions will follow.

One of the seemingly best ways to protect the person who's been hurt a lot is to lie and hide. The temptation is almost irresistible. If you can keep something hurtful from her, she won't get hurt!

Every once in a while, this tactic of lying and hiding works. It works just often enough to keep us doing it.

And that's why people who've been hurt end up being lied to.

But this is a terrible tactic, far more destructive in the long run than the alternative. That's because the truth almost always comes out. And for someone who's been hurt, being lied to or deceived is far worse than almost anything else.

So even if it might cause you some grief in the short run, be as honest and open as possible. Every little bit of hiddenness, exaggeration, or distortion will feed the beast. You want to starve the beast to death.

You understand that you will get some grief for your honesty in the short run. No one likes the bearer of bad news. So you have a little argument. So what? Your always being open and honest will make you a trusted person in the long run and your partner will feel much safer.

Don't make promises you won't keep.
We all fall victim to this. We feel we're being pressured by someone and we want to get him off our back. So we make a promise. "Fine, I'll clean out the closet this weekend." Or, "Fine, I'll talk to my boss about that raise."

We may have the best of intentions, but once we're out of that moment of pressure, the promise suddenly seems less of a good idea. Or it turns out to be less doable.

So you don't keep the promise, and you hope that the other person won't notice or will accept your excuse. Of course, usually the situation takes a very different approach. He's stunned and hurt that you've broken a promise. He feels betrayed.

And as we all know, you soon get into a big fight in which the other person tries to show why this is a huge, big deal and you try to show them why they're crazy not to think it's a little deal. These fights rarely end well.

So when you're dealing with someone who is at all fragile—and honestly, we're all fragile when it comes to feeling betrayed—just do this. Never, ever, make a promise unless you absolutely know that you will keep it. Always underpromise and overdeliver.

Be careful. You may rightly feel that the other person is begging you to give them a guarantee that you will do something. Every part of you may feel that you just want to get this person off your back. It doesn't matter. Don't promise what you won't deliver.

Validate; don't oppose.
Here's a nearly universal error, and it's very destructive. Your partner bursts forth with some fear or grievance involving you. You feel under assault. So you do with your partner what you would probably not do with your friend: You give her an argument. You try to convince her that she's wrong for feeling the way she feels.

And what does that accomplish? All it does is make her feel that you just don't get it, and she feels even more vulnerable.

Suppose she talks about how she's afraid you're going to

cheat on her the way her ex did. If you deal with her fear by say-ing, "That's silly. I would never cheat on you," she's just going to feel you've dismissed her. Which is, of course, what a cheater would do.

Instead, you need to say something like, "I understand. Guys have cheated on you in the past. And there I am out at work all day but you don't know where I am and what I'm doing. I to-tally get it that you're afraid that I might be cheating and you wouldn't even know." Then *ask her* what you can do to reassure her. Let her tell you.

I know that feels as though you were handing her ammuni-tion. But validation like this will always work to rebuild trust.

A hurt person's fears aren't something to be brushed away with a fly swatter. Instead, they're an opportunity for you to show that you take the other person's needs seriously.

Some people are afraid to do this because they think that val-idating the other person means that you're agreeing with their irrational fears.

But you're not agreeing with their irrational fears at all. You're not, for example, saying, "Yes, you're right, I am going to cheat on you." No, you're really just saying, "I understand that you feel this way, and I understand why."

Accept that the other person doesn't feel safe.

The temptation is almost irresistible. At some point you will feel like screaming, "Stop it! I'm not Ann, Mary, Isabel, or any of the other girls who hurt you. I'm me and I'm not going to hurt you. So cut it out."

As tempting as this is, it's a mistake. The other person will eventually feel safer but it can only happen when he's ready. If you tell him to stop before he's ready he's just going to hear that you don't want him to be the way he is. Accept the fact that part of the price of being with this person is how easy it will be for him to feel unsafe when something comes up that stimulates his suspicion.

Think of it this way. When you're with someone who's been hurt in the past, you have the (probably) lifelong task of being there for him as he is. It would be nice to think that you will never hurt him, but it's impossible to completely avoid hurting someone you care about. If you can show that you're there for him, which means accepting him the way he is, then you've done the best a person can do.

Success.

It's important to think of the upside. Yes, there are challenges that come with being with someone who's been hurt in the past. But there are rewards as well, most of all the tremendous gratitude the other person will feel that you're not one of those people who hurt her.

Understand what success here consists of. It's not about being perfect. It's about being honest and understanding and supportive, and it's about avoiding all unnecessary hurt. That's very doable. And when you do that, you can heal the other person's mistrust.

WHAT ABOUT PARANOIA?

Every once in a while, we find ourselves involved with someone who has a suspicious personality. She's mistrustful by nature.

She assumes that everyone, including you, is out to get her. It's just a question of when.

How do you know that you're with someone like this? There are two major signs. The first is obvious: She's very suspicious. You always feel her mistrust or the possibility of it.

The second sign is important. *It's that there's nothing you can do to overcome her mistrust.* You can be literally perfect and she still won't trust you.

In other words, a suspicious person isn't that way because of anything you do or because of anything that was done to her in the past. You didn't make her that way. And you can't prevent her from being that way.

Now here's what makes this confusing. The suspicious person may very well have been hurt in the past, and if so she's likely to point to those hurts as a reason for her suspicion. So what's the difference between someone who's merely been hurt in the past and someone who has a suspicious personality?

The difference is that someone who's been hurt in the past can be reassured. She can learn to trust. In fact, she wants to trust. It's just hard for her.

But the suspicious person's *agenda* is to be mistrustful. Her mistrust isn't a response to you or to what's happened to her in the past. It's part of her identity. In a weird way, she wants to be mistrustful. A part of her even thinks of it as being smart.

So what does this mean for you? I'm all about restoring trust in your relationships, but I have to say it's very unlikely to happen when you're dealing with a suspicious personality. What's most likely, instead, is that you'll be sucked into a vortex of bitterness and anger. You'd be better off ending the relationship. That's pretty stark, I know. Fortunately, for most of us that doesn't apply. Most suspicious people aren't that way because they have suspicious personalities. It's not paranoia but life experience that fills people with suspicion. And that's good news.

HOPE FOR THE FUTURE

THE GOOD NEWS is that we can learn from experience.

For some of us, that learning is all about how we can be hurt. And that's too bad. But we can also learn that these hurts can heal. We can learn that there are people out there who are far less likely to hurt us. We can learn about how resilient we are. We can learn that trust makes sense. We can learn how to create the solidly based trust we're so hungry for.

17

A Life Opened Up by Trust

YOU ARE NOW, believe it or not, a different person than you were when you started this journey with me. It's not only that you have a set of tools and insights that you never had before. You can also see before you possibilities you may have never dreamed of. Or maybe you had those dreams and for a while they were dashed, but now they're possible again.

You've always known that it was all about trust. Now you know how to bring trust back into your life. Not just trust as a feeling or a blind leap of faith, but trust that makes sense and is solidly based.

I've shown you how to make all this happen. It's not really all that hard. You already have everything you need to be able to do it. All you ever needed was someone to show you what mistakes to avoid, and now you have that.

You and the other person now have a map for the journey

back to each other and all the tools for making that journey. This is a journey that will change your life. It's like losing a fear of flying. Not only is being in a plane easier, but the whole world it opened up to you. With your being able to trust people you care about, not only will your relationships feel better but the whole world of love and intimacy and affection and closeness will be fully open to you.

I wish you the best. Please visit me at www.MiraKirshenbaum .com and let me know how your journey back to trust turns out. I'd love to hear from you.

Suggested Topics for Discussion Groups

Since trust is such a hot-button topic for so many of us, this book should lend itself very easily to book clubs and discussion groups.

Here's a list of just some topics for discussion just to get you started:

- Whom do you trust and why?

- Whom don't you trust and why?

- Whom did you used to trust that you don't anymore? What happened?

- Who trusts you and why?

- In what ways do you and don't you trust yourself and why?

- What's the worst betrayal you've ever experienced?

- To what extent have you been able to recover from that betrayal?

- What would you consider to be an unforgivable breach of trust?

- Why do you think there is so much mistrust in our society, and what do you think can be done about it?

- Can you imagine a situation in which there was perfect trust and yet there were still problems in communication?

- Have you ever experienced a situation in which there was a breach of trust and yet the mistrust healed quickly, easily, and naturally? How did that happen?

- Out of all the mistakes covered in this book, which of them have you seen violated in your relationships?

- Whom do you know who is seriously mistrustful because of what's gone on in her previous relationships, and how has this affected this person?

- Talk about ways in which you've seen power imbalances affecting trust in relationships.

- Talk about ways in which you've seen differences in backgrounds affecting trust in relationships.

Acknowledgments

I am grateful to all of you—patients, friends, interviewees, colleagues, and others—who trusted me with your stories of some of the most difficult moments in your lives. You betrayed someone or had been betrayed by someone. The hurt and shame you felt were enormous. And yet you shared your feelings and memories with me, trusting that this would somehow help others. And your trust has borne fruit: you're holding the result in your hands.

It was all of you who taught me—suspicious me—that it really is all about trust. Trust is a mystery: a leap into the dark that is absolutely necessary if we're to be safe and happy in this crazy world. Trust is so fragile, because we're so imperfect and so easily hurt. But it's the most important thing, because without trust nothing good can happen in our lives.

I particularly want to thank everyone who participated in the research for my book *When Good People Have Affairs*. Of course affairs are only one of the many ways trust is damaged in relationships. You showed me that even here, when the pain and damage can be so great, trust can be restored and relationships can come back to life.

That's the challenge, isn't it? To keep trust alive—even though it's so easily broken.

And I want to thank all of you who asked me—begged me, actually—to follow up my book on affairs with a book on how to restore trust in a relationship after a betrayal.

And a special thanks to those who said, "…and remember, there are many more kinds of betrayal than just affairs."

You're right. That's what makes this book so important. This is the first and only book that shows the principles for restoring trust after any kind of betrayal. We need this, because unfortunately betrayals big or small are pretty much inevitable in human relationships. Fortunately, based on our research and that of so many others, we now know that broken trust can heal, and it can heal faster and more easily than many of us have thought.

I've been with my brilliant agent, Howard Morhaim, for more than sixteen years now, and we've done eleven books together. That's one book every year and a half. And that's a big Wow! Howard, you're the best. And many thanks also to Katie Menick, Howard's associate, for all you've done in support of my work.

Huge thanks to Danny Baror, my wonderful international agent, for making it possible for my books to appear in so many lands and languages.

Many heartfelt thanks to my extraordinary editor, Denise Silvestro, for all your passion, wisdom, and commitment to this book. It wouldn't have happened, and wouldn't have been as good, without you. It's been a pleasure to work with you. Thanks also to Meredith Giordan for all your supportive contributions.

And tremendous thanks to Craig Burke for your energy and support, to Julia Fleischaker and Liz Keenan for all you have done and will do to bring this book to people's attention, and to all the other people in publicity at Penguin.

I am also very grateful to my managing editor, Pam Barricklow, and to Erica Rose, who copyedited the book, and to all the people at Penguin whose proofreading and other essential work has been so professionally and excellently done.

Heartfelt thanks to the team here at the Chestnut Hill Institute. You guys—Nikki Green, Doc Miner, Lindi Flanagan—have helped me so much with research, training, outreach, supervision. I couldn't have done it without you.

And a special thanks to our incredibly talented webmaster, Christine Harbaugh.

I am especially grateful to my husband, Dr. Charles Foster. He was unbelievably brave and generous in being willing to let his story be among the many stories told here.

But Charles is more than just my husband—he is my writing partner. We told this story, and wrote this book, together. In every book that's come out under my name I have acknowledged how he is the full, fifty-fifty partner in the writing of the book. That was true then and it is true now with *"I Love You but I Don't Trust You."* But since we're talking about trust here, I should say that this "fifty-fifty" stuff isn't just a polite expression. The truth is that in this as in every book under his or my name we sit down and write the book together. Every word and thought is just as much his as it is mine.

Finally, my mother. I've talked about her a number of times in my books. She died six months ago. There's so much to say, but this is a book about trust and hope and that's what I want to focus on here. I talk in this book about how tough times growing up made it hard for me to be an easily trusting person. And that's true. But there is another way of looking at it. Given the tough times we went through I am in fact a remarkably trusting and hopeful person. I have in me a deep security I've only just begun to appreciate.

And I got that to a very large extent from my mother. I was the daughter of a very tough, smart woman. She, mostly on her own, kept my brother alive during the Holocaust, and then kept me and my brother alive and well in the difficult years after the war when we were refugees and penniless immigrants. She brought us to America and gave us a great life. Everything I have builds on the platform she built. Growing up the daughter of someone with her strength and brains and accomplishment gives you a deep, deep confidence that you can survive, that at the very least you can always trust yourself.

This was a huge and special gift. My mother didn't have the power to make life easy and safe. But she did give me the imperishable gift of knowing that trust makes sense. And no gift is more important than that. It is my mother who made me, and this book, possible. I'm deeply grateful beyond words.

If you have any comments or questions, if you need help, or if you just want to read my blog, please visit me at www.MiraKirshenbaum .com.

Ready to find
your next great read?

Let us help.

Visit prh.com/nextread